PERSONAL FINANCE SECRETS FOR YOUNG ADULTS

101 FINANCIAL LITERACY TIPS TO HELP YOU REDUCE DEBT, CHOOSE INVESTMENTS, UNDERSTAND MONEY MANAGEMENT, ACHIEVE YOUR FINANCIAL GOALS, AND RETIRE EARLY!

JULIAN PAUL

CONTENTS

Based On True Events

INTRODUCTION

The Root

Success is nothing more than a few simple disciplines,
practiced every day; while failure is simply a few errors in
judgment, repeated every day. It is the accumulative weight of
our disciplines and our judgments that leads us to either
fortune or failure.

—Jim Rohn

"How many of you want the freedom to do what you want
when you want to? Yes or yes?"

"Yes..." A few people murmur from the dimly lit crowd.

Sitting in the back of the room, leaning far back in my chair, I
slowly inch my butt lower on the thin pad of the hard plastic
chair, leaning way back in my seat in the hotel conference
room. I make sure my eyes can just barely peer over the top of
the heads within the sparsely populated audience.

"I've got news for you..." continues the presenter, the third speaker of the night by this point. It is getting late.

"Lack of money is never a problem," he pauses for impact.

What is this guy talking about? I think to myself. *The flyer said this seminar was supposed to be all about real estate. This ain't real estate!*

"Yes, it's true. Lack of money is NEVER the problem... It's only the result!"

By now, I am slouching all the way down in my seat, eyes half-closed, notepad and pen casually falling out of my lap as I literally begin to fall asleep.

"If lack of money is only the result, then we don't need to worry about results, right?" The speaker goes on, raising his hand after every statement.

"We need to figure out what the ROOT cause of the problem is. Are you with me?" (Hand Raise)

Suddenly, something the speaker says strikes me like a lightning bolt.

I blink a few times, sit up a little straighter in my seat, and furrow my eyebrows with intensity. *Root cause of money issues? Is that even a thing?*

"If you shoot for the stars, you'll at least hit the moon..." the speaker elaborates. "Most people never shoot for the ceiling in their house, and wonder what the problem is! Are you with me?" (Hand raise)

It occurs to me this speaker is talking about a *mindset* towards money.

This marks the first time in my young adult life that I have ever heard anyone speak about money in terms of how you think. Sidenote: It would be another three years before I'd learn about the book *Think and Grow Rich*.

Sitting in my chair in this random seminar, a recent college graduate, living broke, paycheck to paycheck, still figuring out my next steps in life, it had never occurred to me that my *mindset* about money was something to pay attention to.

As I consider it, the concept makes a lot of sense to me.

As an athlete, my high school and college coaches would sprinkle in "mental training" exercises, and rather than doing anything physical, we were told to use our mind only.

Focus on seeing myself making the play, visualize the statistical achievements for the season, or even use the power of the mind, also known as mental toughness, to heal myself faster from injuries.

What started out as weird imagination exercises had proven beneficial in my life. Nowhere was this more evident than in my senior year of high school when I healed myself from a catastrophic injury. This injury occurred in the very first game of the season, leaving me unable to walk the next day. In fact, I had to use my grandmother's walker to get from class to class that week.

Not only did I learn to walk again, I played every game that season, eventually leading my team to a division championship.

If I could apply this thinking to sports, why couldn't I apply it to money?

As the speaker concludes, he gives the audience a book titled "The Millionaire Mind" by author T. Harv Eker and two free tickets to an upcoming Millionaire Mind Workshop.

~

There came a point in my student life when I decided I was done with formal education. This was it. I was ready to take the next steps, regardless of where the path would lead.

While sitting in that initial seminar, a college (soon-to-be) graduate who did not have a clear idea of what was to come, I felt a sense of the freedom and excitement that only comes from the realization that now the time has finally come for me to direct my own path in life.

No more classes and hours of lectures. No more midterm exams, study hall cramming sessions, and pulling all-nighters just to pass. No more counselors and professors to guide me on what class to take next, or which chapter to read from the textbook.

Although I would dearly miss the benefits of joining various clubs, playing sports, and having a diverse set of uber-talented and intellectual friends, the time had come to take on a new adventure. The next chapter was beginning.

It was time to make the leap from student to young professional!

I was now ready to take on all of life's challenges, and deep down I knew I would succeed.

Unknowingly, one thing I did not understand about the journey into being a young adult was the importance of sound money management.

This was completely off my radar.

In my youth, I learned a lot about history, algebra, biology, statistics, psychology, computer science, and building a great resume. Yet, I had no concrete plans or idea of how to use money to prepare financially for the road ahead.

I knew very little about budgeting, investing, credit cards, or saving for emergencies. Instead, I spent and saved money with no exact formula or reasoning.

For example, when I decided (on a whim) to buy a stock, I put a chunk of my savings into one stock (Apple), and that was it. Or, when my bank offered me a CD with what they described as an attractive interest rate, I would take another chunk of money and lock it into the CD for 6-months just to try it out.

The path I chose was laden with pitfalls and landmines, and my fool-hardy spirit clumsily tripped over several of these landmines before I finally had enough and made a concerted effort to figure out the game I was playing.

Unfortunately, many adults will never overcome money pitfalls, as statistics show that only one-third of adults worldwide understand basic financial concepts.[1]

Make no mistake about it—once you finish high school, the world treats you like an adult. This is the stage where you can sign your own contracts, rent a car, apply for loans, and even get married without parental consent.

Many high school and college graduates feel very ill-prepared for this level of responsibility.[2]

That's why many "professional students" never want to leave school, prefer to spend years getting degrees, and never branch out from the shelter of academia.

Unfortunately, leaving school and rushing out into the "real world" isn't always the best route either.

Throughout this book, you will learn the story of how I went from being a green and gullible college graduate to building success as a financial services professional and what I learned throughout the process. This book contains all the key lessons I discovered about money.

You will learn the truth about the "not-taught-in-schools" missing education at the crux of it all: financial literacy.

Consider this book as your vocational course into adulthood — your Money School 101B.

Throughout the chapters, I'll go through the most essential concepts that will help you make the best financial decisions, which include:

- Quickest ways to eliminate bad debt
- Creating a private pension for retirement
- Importance of credit and how to improve it
- The Old versus NEW Three-Legged Stool
- How to hack your investment returns
- Using debt to propel your financial freedom
- Secrets about how taxes work
- And so much more.

If you've read our first book, *Personal Finance for Teens and College Students*, you will remember the story where I explain how I managed to graduate from college financially illiterate.

But I didn't truly realize my plight until I started a career in the financial industry.

You may be wondering about the journey. What are the real secrets that enabled me to overcome my financial hurdles?

What about the resources that you can use to improve your personal finances?

The teachers, courses, products, and so forth?

Never fear, my friend!

It's all inside this book.

I'm going to show you what it takes to seamlessly transition from being a student or postgraduate with no idea about finances to being a young adult equipped with the knowledge and resources to put your money in the right place(s) from the beginning.

By the end of this book, you will be an amateur turned Pro.

Join me in chapter one, where I reveal my first life-changing epiphany.

I

THE START

"Don't let someone who gave up on their dreams talk you out
of yours."

—John Assaraf

"Congratulations to this year's graduating class!"
said the voice over the loudspeaker as cheers
broke out all around the stadium.

We took off our caps and threw them high in the sky, not
knowing where they might land. Some of my classmates spent
hours decorating their outfits and kept their caps tightly fitted
on their heads.

We jumped and gave our neighbor a midair high-five, smiling,
beaming pearly white teeth. O, what a memory it was!

This momentous occasion had families flying across the entire world to see their children graduate college. In fact, this event just happened several months ago.

But as I sit in the living room (turned bedroom/office), staring off into space, reminiscing, it seems like this graduation ceremony happened ages ago.

Life after college was supposed to present me with grand accomplishment after grand accomplishment! The entrepreneurial journey was to effortlessly present me with rapid success within one or two months. That was my destiny!

But no.

Here I am, now in month 6 of the journey, and still don't have the success to show for all the smarts and quick wit that helped me cruise through schooling. It has not been bringing the same results in this new reality.

I adjust one of the pillows on the frat house couch (also known as my bed) and move my wallet from the sofa cushion to my JanSport backpack. The wallet reminds me of the credit card within and how close the card was to being maxed out. *Just keep making those minimum payments.*

It dawns on me that I have to leave soon to make it to my part-time job. With sixty minutes remaining, I decide that I must do something productive. The rest of my day would be spent at the job, and I cannot waste the opportunity worrying about lack of money.

That's it! I should look up that thing... what was it again? Oh yea, something like Millionaire Brain... no, Millionaire Mind!

I stare off into the distance, momentarily distracted by the life-sized cutout of a famous WWE superstar in the house. One of my frat brother's admiration with this wrestler grew so intense that this poster board became a mainstay in the living room.

I direct my attention back to the task at hand. *Ok Julian, set a timer, look up Millionaire Mind and let's try to learn something before we go.*

As I follow the instructions given to myself, I come across a recording from a funny-sounding man named T. Harv Eker where he is speaking before a live audience.

"Rich people play the money game to win," Eker professed while resting his arms on the podium. "While the poor and middle class play the money game trying *NOT* to lose." There was a pause as the realization struck home. "If your goal is just to be comfortable folks, chances are you'll *never* be wealthy. But if your goal is to be wealthy, chances are you'll be <u>very</u> comfortable!" Laughter and claps from the crowd.

The video then progresses to Mr. Eker describing a money system he designed, which worked extremely well for himself and his participants. This money system is simply named as the "Jar Method".

This is a process of splitting income into six separate piles (or "jars") every check before spending a dime. The jars are intended for specific purposes. For this method to have the most impact, Mr. Eker implores participants to actually use physical cash and place the money into something tangible, such as jars, envelopes, vases, etc.

The jars[1] are split as follows:

50% of income for Necessities, 10% for Financial Freedom, 10% for Long-Term Savings, 10% for Education, 10% for Play, and

10% for Giving/Charity. The detailed categories are explained below:

1. **Necessities:** These are the things that need to be paid for each month, regardless of circumstance. Necessities include things such as bills (including mortgage, rent, internet, cell phone, insurance, etc.) and also include money for food, gas, and other groceries. If 50% of your income is too low to cover your necessities, you should work on lowering expenses and/or increasing your income.

Note: Whatever percentage of income you have left after necessities (or if necessities take up much more than 50% of income), continue to divide that amount into the other jars as best as possible.

2. **Financial Freedom:** This money gets separated out FIRST from your income. This is your nest egg, and it is meant to be used as an asset that will increase in value over time. This jar (also called the Financial Freedom Account or FFA) is used for building wealth. You never spend the money in this jar; you only utilize it for investments and other means to develop more profits.

3. **Long-Term Savings (LTSS):** This jar is used for lump sum spending. Even though this category has the word "savings", it is actually meant to be _spent_ once the target amount has been saved. That's why the name of this account is LTSS (or Long-Term Savings for _Spending_). Try to pick something that would require 3-6 months of savings (i.e. car repairs, weekend vacation, new furniture, theme park visit, or

even a debt paydown), and save 10% of your income each month into this jar. Once you reach the target amount needed for the expense, spend this entire jar on that and reap the rewards of your well-established good money habits.

4. **Education:** Use this money for any personal and professional development. This includes seminars, workshops, courses, etc. As a wise person once said: "The more you learn, the more you earn."

5. **Play:** Spend the money in this jar each month. Treat yourself each month to something, and spend this money freely. It can be a dinner, treat, clothes, meal upgrade, new bag, or anything else you can imagine. Do not save any money from your play month-to-month; do your best to use this jar each month.

6. **Give (a.k.a. Charity):** This final jar is used for tithing and/or charity. Use this jar to make donations, provide gifts to others, and bless your community in whatever way you choose.

After explaining how to start this money system, Mr. Eker asks if anyone from the audience has any feedback to share. As a microphone is handed to volunteers from the crowd, a few participants share their surprising results after implementing this money system in their lives.

One woman's testimonial stands out to me. She expresses how this jar method "alone" helped her get out of debt and become set for life, and she never has to worry about money again.

Really? This is it?!? I begin contemplating how much I can start putting into jars.

As a young kid, I was not taught anything about money management. Now, at this brand new stage in my life, fresh out of school and entering the adult world, this jar technique feels like gold to me.

After a few calculations, I realize I will need over 120% of my income to cover my basic necessities.

"Turn to your neighbor, give him a high-five, and say, 'You have a Millionaire Mind!'" the voice on my computer screen says.

I turn off my laptop in a fit of frustration. *I can't even use that method!*

Beep Beep….*Beep Beep*….*Beep Beep* sings the cell phone timer, reminding me that it's time to leave the house.

I quickly organize all my belongings into a disheveled pile in a far corner of the living room. I grab my bookbag and leave the frat house, smacking the WWE cardboard cutout on the way out.

2

WHO GETS PAID FIRST?

"Don't gain the world and lose your soul, wisdom is better
than silver or gold."

—Bob Marley

"And now introducing your commencement speaker,
Mr. T. Harv Eker!" the announcement booms around
the stadium.

Whispers of hushed confusion are exchanged between the
graduates.

"Wait, what the heck! Who the freak is T. Harv Eker?" My
classmate sitting beside me can barely contain himself as he
comments aloud.

"He's the money guy, right?" I try to respond.

"No, are you serious?! I thought we had Oprah this year?" the girl on my other side exclaims.

As Mr. Eker approaches the podium, several professors give a half-hearted golf clap behind him on the stage. The rest of the stadium gives no cheers at all.

The freshly manicured lawn, which hosts over 1400 students dressed in cap-and-gowns, fall dead silent. Even with all of our parents, grandparents, siblings, aunts, uncles, cousins, and children lining the bleachers, you can hear a pin drop.

Mr. Eker spreads his papers out neatly before him, clears his throat, and stares around the audience for a long, eerie minute.

Suddenly, he shouts at the top of his lungs, "YOU HAVE A MILLIONAIRE MIND!"

In unison, all my classmates shout back, "YOUUUUUU HAVE A MILLIONAIRE MIND!"

"You see, what I've come to tell you today, folks, is that it doesn't matter about your degrees, it doesn't matter about your education! In the real world, which you're about to go out and explore, it only matters about your mindset."

I look over to the classmate who could barely contain himself before and discover he has a pen and pad out taking notes: *T. Harv Eker - Money Mindset* are the words written on the top of his page in blue ink.

"You see, there's a difference between a rich and poor mindset," Mr. Eker continues. "And which mindset do you wanna have, folks?"

"RICH!" The entire stadium yells back on command.

"You see folks, there's so many good ideas I can teach you today on your graduation day, but I only have a few minutes so we'll just focus on one concept today, and that's the concept of results." Mr. Eker walks from behind the podium and begins pacing the stage.

"Let me tell you folks, and some of you aren't gonna like this, but the poor mindset says, 'I get paid based on my time.' Hold on, let me write this down." Mr. Eker stops pacing and appears beside a large easel pad with colorful markers. He grabs a large red marker and writes the word "TIME" in large capital letters.

"Now you know what the wealthy mindset says?" Mr. Eker pauses to switch to a large green marker. "The wealthy mindset says 'I get paid based on my results'... Take notes on this folks!" Mr. Eker writes the word RESULTS in large green letters for everyone to see.

"Are you with me?" Mr. Eker raises his hand high above his head. I notice a few audience members raise their hands in response.

"Now for this next part of my presentation, I'm going to need a volunteer," Mr. Eker looks around the enormous stadium, scanning quickly with his eyes, then barks "Let's go with *You*, over there!" while pointing somewhere behind me.

I turned and looked around at the classmates sitting behind me, trying to figure out who he was calling up to the stage for this random demonstration.

"Yes, you there! The one looking behind himself."

Who? Me?? I start to turn back around to face the front.

Suddenly, Mr. Eker and his sizeable white easel pad are directly in front of me. I stare into his light brown eyes, while Mr. Eker adjusts his microphone headset. "Thanks for volunteering. What's your name?" he asks.

"Uh? Julian.." I mumble curiously.

"Julian, I like that name! Now listen, Julian. I'm going to write an equation here on the board, and I want you to help me out. Can you do that?"

"Sure, Ok." I don't know if I should stand or keep sitting. I stay seated.

Mr. Eker hurriedly jots down an equation that looks like an algebraic formula. *I hope you don't make me solve this in front of all these people.* My armpits sweat a little.

As Mr. Eker finishes writing, I see an equation that looks like **T-F-A=R.**

"Now, can you see what I've written here, Julian?"

"Yes, I can."

"All right, now guess what Julian, class is in session! Not to put you on the spot, but if you had to give your best guess, what does this mean? And don't worry, you've already graduated, there's no failing here!" A couple chuckles sound from behind me.

What the f, this is gibberish! I quickly recall a formula from my freshman year physics class. "Uhhh, this is Temperature minus Farenheit minus..."

"Nice try smarty pants, but let me stop you there Julian," interjects Mr. Eker. "Now this has nothing to do with chemistry. But if you understand this formula, you'll have the key ingredients to experiment your way to success, are you with me?"

"Yes," I nod.

"Are all of you ready to learn this formula?" Mr. Eker stares up into the audience (that I forgot was even there) as cheers sound out all around me.

"Let me ask you a question Julian," Mr. Eker turns his focus back to me. "When you are about to do anything in life, what must happen first?"

"You have to take action," I respond instinctively.

"Well not yet, action comes later, but before you take any action, what do you always do first?"

I hear hushed whispers spring up around me. *I don't know!* I think to myself.

"Like what are you doing right now?" Mr. Eker prods.

"Uhhh, talking... no... Thinking?"

"Right! Exactly! Thinking. So that is the first part of the formula. The *T* here stands for *Thoughts*," Mr. Eker turns back to the easel and writes THOUGHTS -> in big purple letters.

"Everything starts with a thought! No matter whether you wanna take a walk around the block or send a man to the moon, it all starts with a thought folks, are you with me?" Mr. Eker asks while raising his hand.

"After you have a thought, you have an emotion, which is also called a *feeling*." Mr. Eker switches his color and continues to write FEELING -> on the easel with a bulky red marker.

Spontaneously, I am overcome with the urge to solve the riddle, "*Thoughts* lead to *Feelings*, which lead to *Action*, which equals... *Results*?" Nostalgic nights spent watching Wheel of

Fortune with my grandparents have prepared me for this moment.

"Oh wow, outstanding work! Give it up for Julian, folks!" Announces Mr. Eker as the formula magically appears on the board:

THOUGHTS -> FEELINGS -> ACTIONS = RESULTS

Suddenly, as the crowd springs into a chorus of applause, the female classmate sitting beside me jumps out of her seat in a fit of excitement and shouts in a manly voice: "ALPHA STEP, OMEGA STEP, KAPPA STEP, SIGMA STEP, GANGSTAS WALK, PIMPS GONE TALK..."

Hey, that song sounds familiar. Why does her voice sound like that? She sounds like Kanye.

"A.K.A. STEP, DELTA STEP, S.G. RHO STEP, ZETA STEP..." she continues, wholly oblivious to the fact that we were all hanging on T. Harv Eker's every word before her random song.

Heyyyy, that's my ringtone! Wait, am I dreaming?

At once, I emerge from the nap on my bed/couch, in the living/bed room of the frat house. My phone's ringtone is blaring on the floor beside me.

I blink my eyes open and jump back, startled by a chisel-chested figurine-looking man staring at me in biker shorts. *Oh my god, it's just you... cardboard guy!*

"I'M A GET ON THIS TV MOMMA, I'MMA, I'MMA BREAK ISH DOWWWWN! I'MMA..." I reach down from the couch and silence the phone.

I rub my eyes, trying to piece reality back together,

appreciating the fact that my college graduation wasn't happening right now.

"*Hello....hello?*" A low voice speaks beside me. "*Julian?*"

I pop up from the couch and look to where the voice was arising. It occurs to me that instead of ignoring it, I have accidentally answered the call.

"Hello?" I hastily put the phone to my ear.

"Yo, what's up Julian, it's Tim."

"Hey, what's up frat?" I reply as the traditional greeting given to my fraternal brothers.

"You still interested in real estate?" he asks.

"Yes. I don't know anything, I just wanted to hear what you've been up to," I confess. Tim is older than me and looks like he had found his footing after college. To my knowledge he is working in real estate, or I assume he is..

"Ok, look I've been wanting to connect with you, bro. I got this meeting coming up, and there's some people I want to introduce you to? Are you free tomorrow?"

People to introduce me to? Meeting coming up? Man, this sounds like a lot for tomorrow. Plus I work tomorrow! Social anxiety begins to set in for me.

"Uhhh, Tim, can I call you back real quick?"

Click

The sound of me hanging up the phone before he can answer.

~

As we take a pause from storytelling, there is a crucial money lesson that is foundational for all money topics that will be discussed here in this book.

The game of money (including the money system explained at length in the first book *Personal Finance for Teens and College Students*) will only work to your advantage if you have this critical piece of the puzzle.

This money lesson does not plainly reveal itself as a public service announcement that stops time with big bold letters reading: "THIS IS THE MONEY LESSON", and is usually buried behind strange names such as 'The Rule of 72' or '50/30/20 Rule' or other smart-sounding concepts.

For the casual observer, you may think of this as simply how to save money. In fact, I also used to think of these simple money lessons as attempting to show me how to save money. But these lessons actually don't teach *HOW* to save money!

These lessons (or rules) don't even explain WHY to save money. Or even WHEN to save money.

Over time, I've found that the so-called "rules" of money lack quite a bit of knowledge.

But there's a common thread that ties all these concepts together, which, if understood, will greatly benefit you from your attempts at learning these "rules".

And that is *mindset.*

Of course, it is difficult to grasp the meaning of *mindset* by words alone. But mindset is fundamental to having success with money.

In other words, beneath every money lesson you will learn, there must be the correct *mindset* when applying the formula/strategy, in order to make the money lesson work most effectively in your favor.

The best way to explain this idea is by telling you a story...

Out of the 50+ personal finance books I discovered in my life, one classic read was the most refreshing and life-changing for me at the time. This book is *The Richest Man In Babylon* (1926) by George S. Clason.

Even though this book was first published in 1926, The Richest Man in Babylon has many personal finance lessons that are quite relevant to this very day. Throughout the book, Clason gives valuable personal finance advice through a series of digestible and easy-to-understand stories set 4,000 years ago in ancient Babylon (Note: This was an actual city that existed in present-day Northern Africa).

The basic principles of money have remained the same for centuries. The book's central message is that money comes in abundance to those who understand the simple laws governing its acquisition.

All of the stories in the book teach valuable lessons, but in this chapter, I'll share my personal favorite. This is the story from which I learned the strategy that helped me start on my path to making wise financial decisions and building wealth.

While reading this story, pay attention not only to the money lesson itself (how to save money), but pay even closer attention to the *mindset*. When you grasp the mindset, you will have the unspoken, unwritten attitude to imprint this money lesson on your life from now until the end of time.

The story centers around a man named Arkad. He grew up as a poor boy from humble beginnings and rose to become Babylon's richest man alive.

Some of his childhood friends were curious about the source of his wealth. *How did he become the richest man in Babylon?* Arkad was no brighter than them in school; neither had he worked any harder than them at work. While they were all similarly toiling away every day and barely scraping by, how did Arkad rise to prominence?

Arkad's rise to riches seemingly came out of nowhere. There had to be a secret behind this, and his friends were determined to find out. These men and women were sick of struggling to exist, while living in the midst of plenty. So all Arkad's friends conspired together to compel Arkad to honestly reveal the secret to his wealth so they could figure out how to become wealthy themselves.

Upon receiving the desperate request from his friends, Arkad was utterly willing to share his secret with his in friends. In fact, he told them to invite everyone they knew to come back at an appointed time to a theater-sized room (yes, theaters and auditoriums did exist 4,000 years ago!) so that everyone could learn this vital information.

On the day of the gathering, Arkad finally began to tell the particular event that happened to him in his life.

Arkad describes how he began as a scribe, carving inscriptions on stone tablets. While working at this job, he became aware of the disparity between the lavish lifestyles of the wealthy and those of the extremely poor, such as himself, who struggled daily to make ends meet. This caused him to ponder constantly if there was a secret to wealth so he could also claim his share of the good things in life. Arkad wasn't ready to spend his life enviously watching others enjoy the good things of life while he suffered.

Even months later, Arkad had nothing to show for his labor, except dirty fingernails. Even still, Arkad continued to ponder what it would be like to become rich someday.

One day, a wealthy money lender, named Algamish, asked Arkad to deliver an order of inscriptions on an expedited schedule, for which Algamish would pay double the normal price. Arkad took on the job, but underestimated its difficulty.

The job was so challenging that Arkad failed to complete it on time.

Algamish was irate upon his return, and in the spur of the moment, Arkad wisely struck a deal with Algamish. Arkad agreed to stay up all night to finish the work, and in exchange, the wealthy man would reveal the secret to becoming rich.

Despite back pain, headaches, and bleeding hands, Arkad completed the inscriptions by the time Algamish returned in the morning. It was now Algamish's turn to fulfill his end of the bargain.

First, Algamish warned Arkad that he needed to pay close attention to grasp the truth in words spoken, or else he'd think that his night's toil was in vain.

"Yes, tell me what you promised!" Arkad urged.

"I found the road to wealth when I decided that a part of all I earned was mine to keep. And so will you." Algamish said.

Arkad waited for the man to continue spilling the secrets, but as it turned out, Algamish had finished saying everything he wanted to say.

"Is that all?" Arkad asked.

At first, Arkad couldn't believe that was the whole secret to wealth. He thought his entire income was his to keep anyway. But Algamish explained that Arkad did not keep any of his earnings. Instead, he was paying everyone else BUT himself — the seamstress, the landlord, the shoemaker, the meat butcher, etc.

In other words, he was laboring for others and had nothing to show for his hard work.

Algamish suggested that Arkad _keep_ a portion of his earnings, which should be at least 10%, no matter how little he earned.

However, it should also be as much as Arkad could afford, with every coin saved to become Arkad's servant, allowing him to make more coins.

When Algamish took his tablets and left, Arkad thought the advice was reasonable, so he gave it a shot. Arkad paid himself one-tenth of his earnings every time he was paid.

Within no time, Arkad had saved enough to begin investing and multiplying his savings. He made mistakes along the way (read the stories about how he suffered losses due to poor investment decisions, and also spent his investment winnings too soon), but eventually Arkad mastered how to acquire money, keep it effectively, and put it back to work for him.

And the advice to get him there was quite simple. Keep a portion of all your earnings.

Most of us, like Arkad at first, expect detailed and unheard-of strategies when we ask self-made millionaires to share their secrets to wealth. In reality, the simple money laws we all know and dismiss are the essential foundations.

Paying yourself first is one of the most straightforward laws of building wealth that most people know, but still need to apply. You will never have an empty account if you save 10% of your monthly income.

However, don't fall prey to the misnomer that "the more you save, the wealthier you'll be", because this simply is not true. In fact, there are many responsible-minded people who focus on saving and cutting back for decades, only to find out in retirement (much too late) that it seems they don't have enough money to live on, and cannot shake the overwhelming urge to continue saving and cutting back for the rest of their entire life. More on this later.

Even still, learning to save is an essential first step to financial empowerment. So make sure to follow the advice of both Algamish and Arkad. Say to yourself, "A part of all I earn is mine to keep." Say it to yourself in the morning, say it to yourself at night, say it to yourself when you get paid, and say it again when you are about to spend. Repeat this mantra every day until the words become ingrained in your mind. Develop your *money mindset*.

When I first discovered this book, I was usually in a feast or famine mode with my finances. Plus, I had no savings. Fortunately, within a few months of practicing Arkad's teaching, I had $100 saved.

From a negative savings account (let's call it $0) all the way to $100!

This may sound like very little savings, but it meant the world to me at the time. I had $100 that was all mine. It was not being set aside for a trip. It was not being prepared to be gobbled up by a debt payment. This $100 belonged to me.

More than the money, I was developing a new and life-changing mindset.

Within a year, I had $1000 saved.

From $0 all the way to $1000!

Again, this money was not about to go towards buying a new Playstation. It was not going towards a down payment for a new apartment. It was not being set aside for end of the year Christmas gifts for the family. This $1000 belonged to me, and it was mine to keep!

After keeping this up for a while, it dawned on me that I could practice making the money grow.

So I started looking for ways to make my savings work for me and discovered Robinhood. It was a brand new app (no other companies were offering $0 trades at the time), and I began buying stocks.

The story continues into a new adventure from there, and it all started with a simple mindset shift: "A part of all I earn is mine to keep."

This is the first mental attitude for you to develop if you desire lasting success in your personal finance endeavors.

Remove your portion *first*, set it aside in a separate account (or cookie jar), then rearrange your bills and discretionary spending as needed. Even if you're in a situation where you feel that you need 100% (or 200%) of your wages, and it seems impossible to keep any of your income for yourself, make it a habit to pay yourself first.

Similar to Arkad and myself, you'll realize that even after setting the funds aside, you won't feel any shorter of funds than before.

If you are absolutely convinced that you cannot save 10% of your income, you can begin with any amount that feels wise for you. The main goal is to develop a mentality that prioritizes your long-term financial well-being instead of focusing only on immediate needs (like bills).

You must make the portion you pay yourself a mandatory expense, similar to a personal tax you owe yourself after every paycheck. And make sure this tax is no less than 10% of your income.

When you're younger and not earning much, it's easy to cling to the idea that you'll save more when you're older or making more money, however this is usually not the case. In most surveys, retirees have one main message they would pass on to their younger selves: Adjust your habits to save and invest more.

The good news is this doesn't require much thought. Simply pay yourself 10% of every paycheck.

If you have little to no savings, the first step is to build up your emergency fund, which will provide breathing room in case of unexpected expenses or income loss. The COVID-19 global pandemic was a clear example of why having an emergency fund is extremely important. Power outages, snowstorms, and natural disasters are also commonplace.

No one anticipates such occurrences, and this is the nature of emergencies.

Even occupational surprises, such as getting laid off, falling sick for months, or other business losses, happen every year. So what about if/when it happens to you?

It's better to be prepared and never experience such a scenario than to be unprepared and experience such an emergency without any plans.

Once you have cultivated a considerable sum, your mind will begin to venture into other ways to use your money and how to properly invest. As your investments grow, you will experience the power of compound interest. This occurs when your money earns dividends, and then those dividends earn dividends.

The longer your money is allowed to grow, the more significant the impact on your returns.

So where do you keep your emergency fund? Although interest helps to beat inflation, the primary considerations for selecting your emergency savings account are fund safety and liquidity.

How much money is adequate for an emergency fund? The general rule is to save enough money to cover 3-6 months of your monthly expenses. So, calculate your monthly expenses and multiply the total by the number of months you want your emergency fund to last.

Remember that even though this crucial money lesson seems to be referring to saving money, it is much more than that: This is a new *mindset* you are developing.

Once you have ingrained this mindset into your personality, your habits will change, your lifestyle will change, and the results will begin to spill over into other areas of your life that you can't even imagine. Like chemistry, this one change to your formula will provide a whole new result.

In the next chapter, we will expand on this foundation and address how to handle the first trap most people fall into, also known as Money Villain #1 — Debt.

3

PAY DOWN BAD DEBTS QUICKLY

"No matter where you're from or what you've done, you're never stuck in a particular circumstance, relationship, or cycle unless you say you are."

—Russell Simmons

"**D**on't you need like a hundred grand to buy a house?" my fraternity brother Will sits across from me at the table, eating a bologna sandwich, curiously staring at me.

"Nah, no you don't," I field his questions, even though I feel unsure about my answers. "You can buy a house with no money down."

"No money down?!?" my other fraternity brother Keenan hops up from the couch (my bed), and plunges into the dining room where we were eating. "You can't buy a house without money! That ish sound like a freaking scam, bruh."

"No, for real, you can buy houses with no money down!" I retort defensively.

"I agree with you Keenan, every house I've seen for sale wants money in exchange." Will teams up with his favorite roommate. *Of course you're going to agree with your best friend, duh.*

"Yea bruh, the next thing you know, he gone ask for money to join something. If it's 'No Money Down' then why you need to pay anything? That's what you need to be thinking, homie!" Keenan is now standing with his chest puffed out, similar to his favorite cardboard cutout.

"I don't know why I'm defending this, I ain't going to his meeting," I humbly accept defeat against my tag team frat brothers. *How did we end up talking about this?* "I have to work tonight anyway, I can't go."

Suddenly Kanye West starts singing *School Spirit* from my phone in the living room. Someone is calling. And according to the ringtone, they are fraternal.

"I bet you that's him!" Keenan shouts as he sprints to the source of the sound to find my phone. I follow him into the living room as he dives into the couch and plucks the blue nokia from between the couch cushion. "Bruh, you need to upgrade this," he teases as he looks at the black and white screen to discover the caller name. "Yup, it's Tim! You want me to press ignore?"

"Wait, wait, hold up..." I snatch the phone swiftly from

Keenan's busy fingers. "Just let me talk to him. I can just tell him I'm not going."

"Too Late!" Keenan cackles with laughter as I realize he has already pressed the ignore button. Tim's call drops. *Well damn... I could've at least asked him... oh well, nevermind.* I felt anger rise within me, and then a sense of relief.

"You'll be thanking me later bruh," Keenan continues while walking back toward the dining room. "Some people try to convince you of the dumbest things. Like you can do anything without money. You can't!! Need a job, like everyone normal knows that bruh."

I follow Keenan back into the kitchen, wondering how to switch the subject.

"Yeah, you know what's funny!" Will outbursts. "So my uncle he had this business, right, and one time, and it was like three in the morning, and I swear..."

"ALPHA STEP, OMEGA STEP, KAPPA STEP, SIGMA STEP..." Kanye sings in my hands.

It's Tim, calling me back.

He must know I just pressed ignore. I feel an instant sting of embarrassment, and unconsciously press the button to answer.

After staring at the phone for a few seconds thinking what to say, I look up and lock eyes with Keenan who is frantically waving his hands back and forth in front of his throat; the universal 'cut it' signal. I consider it for a moment, then put the phone receiver to my ear, and jog out of the house.

"Hello?!" I bark roughly while exiting the front door.

"Julian, what's up! You coming tonight, man?"

"Coming where?" I feign ignorance.

"Come to my office tonight, bro. I got some people you need to meet."

"Yo, I work tonight. I don't think I can't get tonight off. This is last minute."

"I told you about this yesterday, bro," Tim's voice exudes a huff of exasperation.

"Yea, I completely forgot," I admit.

"Hold up, can I ask you something Julian?"

"Ok? What's up?"

"How long have you had that job?" Tim asks pointedly.

"Uhh, maybe like four years?" I surprise myself with how long it's been.

"Four years, ok!" Tim exclaims. "So first thing, I'm pretty sure you can call in sick for one night." *Well sure, you got me there.* "But also, are you doing what you see yourself doing for the next 20 years? Are they paying you good there?"

"No," I admit again. Now feeling slightly ashamed.

"Just give me one night, bro. I promise you, if you stick with me for four years, the next 20 years of your life will look sooo different!" Tim is speaking with a fervor that I had never heard from him before.

"I'm...uhh... I'm just... You know..." I forget all the good excuses I had rehearsed in my head. "I don't know, frat. It just seems like a lot."

"Wait, I know you got some loans you tryna pay off right?" Tim inquires.

"Umm...sure?" I think about the near-maxed credit card in my wallet.

"Well you can at least learn how to get that paid off quicker."

"Man...alright fine!" I concede. "Text me the address. No promises though, I still gotta call my manager."

~

IN THOSE YEARS, I FELT AS THOUGH I KNEW HOW TO USE MONEY, SINCE I saved and tithed every month. However, my results after the first few months post-college was a credit card debt that kept growing, and my lack of knowledge on how to keep it paid off.

The other idea that plagued my mind was the thought debt was terrible. Like a toxic relationship that was important for me to stay far away from. Yet here I was using it, mindlessly without forethought.

Years later, I would discover that not all debt is bad. Actually certain debt is very good, when used strategically.

Several factors determine whether a given debt is good or bad. The primary factors are the interest rate, the purpose of the loan, the method or system to repay it, and the length of time it you require to payoff the debt.

Most young adults are trained to think of debt as negative, but you will learn that not all debts are created equal.

Good debt goes towards opportunities that help you accumulate long-term wealth or passive income over time. The primary goal of good debt is to increase your wealth capacity or your money flow.

It is easy to see how a lack of sufficient funds prevents you from pursuing new investments, starting new projects, or propelling your ideas into reality.

For instance, you find a great deal on a real estate property because you have a personal connection with a friend or neighbor. You have a well-researched idea to turn the property into a cash machine but don't have the kind of funds needed to take over the property and bring your idea to life. There are a few options available to you:

Option 1: You give up. Resolve that you don't have the money, and can't buy the house yourself. Resign yourself working your job everyday just to make sure the ends meet, and forget all about the deal since you don't know how to come up with that kind of money.

Option 2: You choose to keep the faith in the idea, and make a passionate effort to obtain the property through your sweat equity. Scrape and save every dollar until you save enough cash set aside to execute the purchase. This could be many years or decades later. By this time, your good friend (even if they said they would wait on you) would have likely sold the property to someone else. Or passed away, allowing others in the family to take over the property (they'll try to sell it to someone else at the fair market rates). OR let's say you actually get the money saved up... You finally make the offer to buy the property years later, you realize inflation has caused all the house prices to raise 100% and now your lump sum STILL cannot buy the house (even though it's still a great deal).

Option 3: Alternatively, you could take out a loan today (50-80% of the total amount) and purchase the property as soon as possible. You capitalize on the fact that the prices will not be going any lower, since inflation will increase costs each year. You also give yourself the benefit of paying back the loan with dollars that are *decreasing in value* every year. And if this deal is structured correctly, you will create a cashflow for yourself that will start now. And you weren't forced to scrape and save your way to bring this idea to reality.

Which option would you prefer? Would you rather 1) give up, 2) save tirelessly, or 3) access funding that allows you to execute your ideas while you still have the time, energy and enthusiasm?

Using debt strategically allows you to accomplish your short-term and long-term objectives early on.

When researching the most common examples of *good* debt, you'll find debts relating to student loans, mortgages, and business loans. However, these are not always the best debts in every circumstance. For us, good debt is defined as debt that has the ability to increase your cash flow and net worth.[1]

Whereas, bad debt, on the other hand, decreases your monthly income, and does not provide the opportunity to build your cashflow. Bad debt jeopardizes your current and future financial well-being. Such debt is typically used for instant gratification and purchasing things that will not increase in value, and have no chance of increasing your income.

In most cases, people aren't able to pay this sort of debt back without straining. In the moment, this sort of debt feels helpful because it helps you gratify your desires, but after the high fades, this debt becomes a burden. Common examples of bad debt include department store layaway plans, casino/gambling debt, and other types of consumer debt.

This chapter will concentrate on bad debt. The kind of debt that is difficult to repay, has high interest rates, puts you at risk of bankruptcy, keeps you awake at night, jeopardizes your collateral, and in most cases, limits your access to more capital.

Let me start by confirming to you that you're not alone if you're drowning in bad debt. Most of us have been there, probably more than once. Even successful icons have confessed to their tribulations with bad debt.

That said, you don't have to give up on your future goals and resign to a miserable life due to bad debt. Instead, we need to build your "Bad Debt Elimination Plan" (BDEP) and get your life back on track as soon as possible. That's what this chapter is all about.

There are several methods for effectively lightening the load of bad debt. I'll share tried-and-true BDEP strategies in this chapter, including:

- 0% Balance Transfer Method
- Using DCCs
- Personal Loan Strategies
- Last Resort BK

Keep in mind that each of these strategies are heavily dependent on your specific situation. Each method comes with its own set of benefits and downsides. So, before implementing a BDEP, take your time to read every detail about it, weigh the benefits and drawbacks, and do the math to determine if it's the right move for you.

At least one of these bad debt escape techniques will help you regain control of your finances and achieve the peace of mind you desire as you move towards financial freedom.

TAKE ADVANTAGE OF 0% BALANCE TRANSFER PROMOTIONS

Imagine you are given a 0% interest loan to pay down your debts. If you were given a set period, say 12-18 months, to pay back the 0% interest loan, would this inspire you to pay off a chunk (if not all) of the loan within the given time period? If you answered yes, then you will love 0% balance transfer promotions.

As the name suggests, a 0% balance transfer involves moving debt from your current high-interest card to a new one with a zero interest rate offered on the transferred amount. In short, you will not be charged interest when repaying the balance on the new card for a certain period.

One of the challenging aspects of paying off credit card debt is the high-interest charges, which take up a large portion of the monthly payments. This makes the zero-APR balance transfer strategy ideal if you need short-term relief from high-interest debt payments to pay the debt off faster. It's also a low-cost method of consolidating credit card debt.[2]

How does a balance transfer work?

The primary goal of a zero-APR promotion is to transfer your high-interest debt to another card with a 0% rate. Your debt remains the same, but you will save the money you would have spent on interest payments, making it easier to focus on paying off the balance quickly.

In most cases, you can only transfer the balance to a zero-APR card if the balance is coming from a different bank. You'll need to make sure the zero-APR introductory offer is coming from a different bank than where your current debt is, in order to take advantage of this tactic.

Once the transfer is complete, you will have no debt on your first card and will only be making payments to the new card. You can enjoy the 0% interest payments for the next 6-12 months (or longer depending on the offer).

Many of these balance transfer offers will allow you to use a physical check, and complete the transfer to any bank account of your choice. This works well if you are not able to do the transfer directly to the debt you are trying to paydown.

It's worth noting that the 0% interest rate duration typically ranges from 6 months to two years. Once the 0% APR promotional period expires, the transferred balance is subject to the card's regular interest rate, which could be just as high as the previous debt's interest rate. That's why this strategy works best if you can devise a plan for rapid payoff during the 0% APR promotional period.

When you don't have to pay interest, increasing your monthly payments will pay off the debt faster and easier.

How much money will you save by doing a zero-APR balance transfer?

As with any financial strategy, you must check the numbers to see if the transfer will save you money. You can use a balance transfer calculator online to crunch the numbers. The important factors to consider include:

- Current card's APR

- New card's 0% APR duration (The longer, the better)
- Interest rate after the expiry of the 0% APR period
- Amount of debt you're allowed to transfer
- Your realistic period of payment completion
- Card's annual fees (if any)
- Balance transfer fee

Let's say you owe $4,000 on a card with 16% APR and $150 minimum monthly payments. If you pay the minimum of $150 each month, you will pay over $950 in interest, and it will take around 34 months (nearly three years) to pay off the balance.

Let's suppose you transfer the balance ($4,000) to a card with a 0% APR promotional period of 15 months, a 3% balance transfer fee, and you pay the same $150 monthly. In this case, you'd pay $120 in transfer fees and the balance would be $650 lower at the end of the intro period, which will reduce the interest payments dramatically.

If you prefer a rapid payoff plan, you'd need to make payments of at least $275 a month on the balance transfer card to pay off the entire balance before the promotional period ends. This way, you'd save yourself from paying any interest and finish paying the debt 18 months sooner than if you simply kept the balance on the original card.

Most credit cards charge a balance transfer fee, which is the amount charged for transferring debt from one card to another. This fee is usually 3-5 percent of the transferred balance and is paid upfront. However, some cards do *not* charge a balance transfer fee. Before you choose a card, figure out if there will be a transfer fee, and how much the fee will be to see if it makes sense to proceed with the offer.

For example, if the bank charges a 3% balance transfer fee and your intended transfer amount is $5,000, you'll receive a $150 fee.

The time it takes for the transfer request to be approved depends on the card issuer, but in most circumstances the transfer will be completed within 14 days. You will continue to pay your current or first bank until the transfer is completed.

Choosing The Perfect Introductory 0% APR Balance Transfer Card

You can find a myriad of zero-interest credit cards by quickly searching online. Banks are constantly offering these zero-APRs balance transfers to attract new customers. After all, they prefer you make payments to them instead of their competitors.

To select the best card, you'll need to search online and compare different offers to choose the best. Make sure you read the fine print thoroughly, checking for the crucial details mentioned earlier.

Make sure the 0% APR offer specifically applies to "balance transfers", as there are many 0% intro offers for new purchases in the marketplace, but this is not the same thing as a balance transfer. Many times, you will find promotions that will offer 0% interest rate on balance transfers OR new purchases, but not both. Make sure you are applying for the card which states "0% Balance Transfer APR" or similar.

It's also worth noting that the 0% APR introductory offer doesn't mean the balance will remain interest-free forever. In other words, the 0% APR offer applies only for a limited time. Also, you may have only a tiny window of time to initiate the balance transfer.

For example, you may receive a "12 months, 0% Balance Transfer APR" card, but in the fine print it will outline that you must make the balance transfer within 60 days of receiving the card. If you miss this detail, and try to take advantage of your 0% balance transfer in month 6, the transferred balance will be charged with the regular interest rates. In other words, do yourself a favor, and initiate the balance transfer(s) soon after qualifying for the account.

If you can afford to pay off your debts quickly during the zero-interest period, take advantage of this offer, because it will save you time and money.

If you manage your money well, but find that you have not completed paying the remaining balance at the end of the 0% interest period, you may also wonder, "Why not qualify for a new promotional rate, and transfer the remaining balance to another 0% interest card when times comes?"

There are some technicians out there who can employ this strategy repeatedly each year, using different cards with different banks, constantly shifting their balances to promotional cards and paying 0% interest and minimal fees until they are able to completely payoff the debt.

And there are others who qualify once or twice for a promotional rate, but then need help qualifying for any more after that.

As a word of caution, repeating this tactic too often may signal to lenders that you are a bad credit risk, especially if the debt does not get paid down (or even grows larger), which will impede your ability to qualify for more attractive offers down the line.

Outside of credit card debts, you may also use balance transfers on other loans like car loans and home equity lines of credit. If the loan is nearly paid off, this can be a wise move when you know you can easily pay off the entire balance during the 0% interest period.

WORK WITH A DCC (DEBT CONSOLIDATION COMPANY)

Another BDEP solution to solve a bad debt situation is to work with a debt consolidation company. Debt consolidation companies could be a great resource, especially if the debt seems to be out-of-control.

These companies provide various debt consolidation programs to help you repay your debt faster while saving money. A good debt consolidation company can save up to 35% of your total debt.

Unfortunately, not every debt consolidation company is reputable. Some of them may charge exorbitant fees or make promises they cannot keep, jeopardizing your credit score and overall financial well-being.

As a result, it's critical first to understand how debt consolidation companies operate and the benefits versus the costs of working with them. In this section, we will teach you how to find reputable companies if you decide this option is ideal for your situation and goals.

HOW DEBT CONSOLIDATION COMPANIES WORK

As mentioned earlier, debt consolidation companies offer different types of programs for handling bad debt. Each type of program has its own pros and cons. Understanding how each program works to eliminate your debt and how much money you'll save before you enroll is crucial.[3]

The primary debt consolidation programs offered are:

- Debt Management Plans (DMPs)
- Debt Consolidation Loans
- Debt Settlement

Debt Management Plans

Nonprofit credit counseling organizations typically offer debt management plans. They have debt counselors who assess a client's overall financial situation, including credit reports and bills, to provide personalized guidance on handling the debt.

To get started with a DMP provider, you'll need to find and contact a credit counseling organization. Based on your financial situation, the counselor will provide you with a personalized plan for resolving your debt, including the reasonable amounts you can set aside to achieve the debt pay-off goal.

Once the plan is in place, the counselor will approach your creditor on your behalf to negotiate better terms, which could include a lower interest rate and affordable monthly payments based on your income. If they reach an agreement, you will send an agreed-upon monthly payment to the organization, which will be disbursed to your creditor. Most programs take 3-5 years to complete, but this depends on your debt.

A debt management plan is ideal for someone who can pay their monthly bills but needs assistance developing a better plan and sticking to it to resolve their debts. It's also suitable if you want to combine multiple debts into a single manageable monthly bill with lower interest and payments.

Make sure you check if the credit counseling organization charges a monthly fee for the DMP and any other costs to avoid unpleasant surprises. The amount you save will be determined by the agreement reached between the credit counseling organization and your creditor.

PROS OF DEBT MANAGEMENT PLANS

- Your credit score is not a factor as this is not a loan.
- You will benefit from lower interest rates and monthly payments.
- The organization assists you in developing a manageable budget based on your income and overall financial situation.
- Credit counselors give you financial advice and answer any questions you have.
- You can consolidate debt and end up with a single payment instead of making multiple payments to different creditors.

Cons of debt management plans

- If you miss a payment, your creditor may cancel all of your concessions.
- Most organizations charge a one-time setup fee (usually between $50 and $75) and a monthly service fee, which is an added cost.
- The organization may require you to discontinue

using credit cards and only keep one emergency credit card.

Debt Consolidation Loans

Some debt consolidation companies offer debt consolidation loan programs. Typically the companies don't provide the loans themselves. Instead, they will connect you with lenders and assist you in choosing the best offers.

Debt consolidation loans help to combine multiple high-interest debts into one monthly payment with a reduced interest rate. Depending on the terms of your new loan, you can get lower interest rates which will help you save money and pay off the debt faster.

Pros of debt consolidation loans

- You can get lower interest rates and lower monthly payments.
- You will make a single monthly payment, eliminating the stress of multiple due dates.
- A fixed repayment schedule ensures that you pay down debt faster than if you only pay the minimum on various high-interest credit cards.

Cons of debt consolidation loans

- You may have to pay a fee upfront.
- The option is ideal only if you can afford to make monthly payments.

- A large loan with favorable terms necessitates good credit.

DEBT SETTLEMENT PROGRAMS

Although most debt settlement programs promote this service as debt consolidation, it is a one-of-a-kind program. These programs are designed for people who are already behind on their payments or have defaulted on their debt. You will typically hear about this program from debt settlement companies and debt settlement attorneys.

A debt settlement program will require you to *stop* paying your minimum monthly payments on your debt, even if you're not behind already. Instead, you will open a dedicated savings account with the company and make a monthly payment to it.

Once you've fallen behind on your bills for a while (usually after six months of saving), the program will negotiate with your creditors to settle your outstanding debts for less than you owe. If they reach an agreement, you will pay the creditor the agreed-upon amount from that savings account. You will also pay the debt settlement company a predetermined fee for their services.

This program offers a way out for those who are already behind on their bills.

PROS OF DEBT SETTLEMENT PROGRAMS

- You'll pay less money overall if the negotiations are successful.

- It saves a significant amount of time on repayment.
- Provides debt relief while assisting in faster repayment.
- If the company negotiates well with the creditor(s), your accounts can be prevented from being sent to collections.

Cons of debt settlement programs

- The period you stop making your monthly payments can hurt your credit score as it's based on payment history. As a result, this program makes more sense if you need to catch up on payments.
- The program may charge a higher fee than the earlier strategies mentioned.
- Your debt forgiveness amount may be taxed.
- Stopping your monthly payments may result in additional fees, interest, and other actions from your lenders, such as debt collection and lawsuits.
- The creditor may reject your settlement offer.
- You may encounter fraudsters who take your money but provide no genuine service in return.

Always look for a company with a good reputation, a transparent process, accreditation, and reasonable fees. Some of these companies will also promise to charge no upfront fees unless they successfully reduce your debt.

TAKE OUT A PERSONAL LOAN

Using one loan to pay off other loans may seem

counterintuitive, but read on to find out how this may be the perfect strategy, depending on the situation.

Personal loans typically have lower interest rates than credit cards, especially if you have a good credit score. This loan will assist you in converting bad debt into better debt by consolidating multiple, high-interest loans into a reduced single payment. After taking out a personal loan to pay off credit card debt, most people are able to pay off their debts faster with lower monthly payments.

To start the process of repaying bad debts with a personal loan, simply look into getting pre-approved for several loan options. It's essential to search for pre-approvals, so the applications won't hurt your credit score as you decide which offer works best for you.

Out of the best offers received, choose your favorite, and submit an application. After approval, use the funds to pay off the bad debts, then use the same money that used to go towards the bad debts, and put that towards paying off the loan each month. The personal loan should decrease much quicker, and your debt will be paid off faster.

Before starting this, realize that taking out a personal loan to pay off bad debt has its own set of advantages and disadvantages, just like any other strategy.

Pros of paying bad debt with a personal loan

- You can pay off your debt in full. While a personal loan will not make you debt-free, it will help you clear all of your bad debt and provide financial relief from having multiple lenders.

- You can obtain a lower interest rate and save significant money on interest charges. Although many factors influence your exact interest rate (such as credit score, loan amount, and other loan terms), personal loans have much lower APRs than credit cards.
- Your debt will be consolidated into a single monthly payment. Having a single monthly payment allows you to better plan your finances and feel more in control of your financial situation. Remember that the more money you contribute to your repayment, the more money you'll save in interest charges over time.
- A personal loan increases your overall credit mix and credit card consolidation lowers your credit utilization (how much of your available credit you're using) on the cards to zero. The ideal credit utilization is below 10%. Your payments on the personal loan will go to your credit report. Thus all these changes affect your credit score positively.

Cons of a personal loan

- There may be a larger minimum amount to pay per month (compared to credit card minimums). You'll need to pay this monthly amount on the personal loan, although at a lower interest rate.
- Personal loans are considered non-revolving debt, meaning you can only use the money once. Any money you use to pay down the loan cannot be accessed again (unlike credit cards and lines of credit).
- You may be unable to obtain low interest rates and/or any personal loans in general if you have bad credit.

- Typically there are fees associated with personal loans, such as origination fees, late payment fees, and insufficient funds fees. Become familiar with the fees associated with your personal loan to avoid any surprises.

Can you get a personal loan with bad credit or no credit?

Getting approved for a personal loan with bad credit is difficult because creditors lack confidence in your ability to repay them on time. And, for the lenders who approve your loan application, it may come with higher interest rates and smaller loans in the amount of $2000 or less.

This may not sound very attractive if you are aiming to get one personal loan to cover all debts, but are only offered a loan that barely covers one-tenth of the debt. Although the amount is minimal, it may still be advantageous to obtain a small loan, use the loan to pay down a portion of the debt, payoff the loan, and repeat.

Also, another benefit of using smaller loans is that you create trust with the lender. After that first debt is paid off, you can re-apply for a larger amount and have a greater chance of approval.

There is another excellent option for those with bad credit, outside of obtaining a personal loan. Instead, you can obtain a secured line of credit to replace high-interest debts. Banks and financial institutions will extend a revolving line of credit secured to an asset such as cash, real estate, equipment, stocks, etc.

For example, if you have $10,000 saved, you can put the $10,000 into a Certificate of Deposit (CD), and open a $10,000 line of credit at the same bank, and they will use the CD as collateral.

The benefits of doing this is there are no/low qualifications for approval. You can get approved for this with a low credit score and no income requirements. Since the Line of Credit is secured, it will have a very low interest rate.

This is just one example, be sure to ask around to find ideas, you will be surprised at what is available.

Having a challenged credit profile and a low credit score will not stop you from getting a personal loan. All it takes is some creative thinking and you will fnd out more ways to qualify for a smart way to smother bad debt.

Here are some additional tips to build up your credit profile and make yourself attractive to lenders.[4]

Check your credit

Before approaching lenders, review your credit report and fix critical errors. Lenders usually require a minimum credit score for loan approval, and you'll know where you stand as you monitor your scores. Having a detailed look at your credit behavior will help you to identify errors, which, after corrected, will boost your score.

The main two ways to improve your credit score is by 1) making all payments on time, and 2) having a long credit history of 7-10 years. These two factors alone affect 50% of your FICO score!

If you have little to no credit history, and have been missing payments, there are still methods for you to clean your credit reports relatively quickly.

For missed payments, see if you can work with the lender to remove missed payments from your credit profile. If the lender won't work with you, it may be wise to have the account removed from your credit profile if you can find a proper dispute (consult a credit repair specialist or find one on YouTube who can give more details).

For those with little to no credit history, become an authorized user on the credit cards of someone with a long, perfect history (preferably 7-10 years of timely payments). You can find a loved one willing to do this, or find someone online, through a reputable website such as tradelinesupply.com.

Once you have prepared your credit profile to apply for credit or a loan, here are a few tips that will help make your process easier:

1. **Take time to compare offers and lenders**

The loan approval requirements differ from lender to lender. Shop around, then pick up the phone, and call them to ask additional questions about their approval requirements. During your research process, you may find one lender who is very lenient with their qualification process versus another. Or, you may discover the credit union you belong to has a special promotion. Or, you may find a particular lender to be very non-responsive and vague. The time you invest in your research now will save you much trouble and confusion down the road, and help you uncover the best rates and terms.

Avoid certain types of personal loans, such as merchant cash advances and payday loans. They may seem appealing because they are easier to qualify for with bad credit, but they have terms that make it easier to increase your debt, rather than decrease it.

High interest rates and shortened repayment periods can make the payments unaffordable, and when the payments start adding up, you may find yourself borrowing again. Be sure to do research and avoid that scenario.

2. Take advantage of prequalification

Most lenders provide online pre-qualification services. You will only need to provide a few details to determine your chances of qualifying for a loan. Pre-qualification is beneficial because it usually registers as a soft-pull on your credit profile, which does not affect your scores.

Typically, lenders will perform a hard credit check when you apply for a personal loan, which *will* (temporarily) lower your credit score. This is also known as a hard inquiry in the credit world. Also, lenders will rate you less favorably the more hard inquiries they find on your credit profile, especially if they are all within a 6-12 month time period.

Therefore, if your application is rejected by one lender, you'll be applying for other loans with a lower credit score and more hard inquiries than you started with, making it more difficult to qualify. Prequalifications will reduce the amount of hard credit checks on your profile, so you can have a higher chance of getting approved when you apply.

3. Add value to your application

Additional options to qualify for a personal loan with low

interest rates are 1) add a co-borrower with good credit to your application, and 2) apply for a secured loan.

A co-borrower with good credit (also known as a "credit partner") will help your credit application stand out. Since the other person's credit score and income are considered for approval, the chances are much higher that lenders will approve a co-signed loan. Keep in mind that if you miss payments, the other person's credit will be negatively impacted. And in case of loan default, the co-borrower is held equally responsible.

On the other hand, another idea is the secured loan, which requires you to put up an asset as collateral. This could be something of value such as your car or a savings account. Lenders look at secured loans more favorable than unsecured loans because the lender knows they can recoup any losses from the value of your asset. If you fail to repay the loan, the asset can be seized. This is why secured loans provide very attractive interest rates.

FILE BANKRUPTCY

Common knowledge says declaring bankruptcy is the absolute worse thing you can do for your credit score. The way people speak about bankruptcy makes it feel similar to lighting a match and burning your credit profile to the ground.

Bankruptcy is like that ugly scar that stays on your credit profile forever.

TEN WHOLE YEARS!

And after that ten years is over, then you have to start ALL OVER again. That sucks.

What if you want to apply for a credit card in the next ten years. Denied!

What if you want to apply for a mortgage and buy a home in the next ten years? Denied.

What if the car breaks down and you need a loan to buy a new/used one? Denied!

With this mindset, there is almost no good reason to get a bankruptcy. If anyone even mentions the word "bankruptcy" you should go Running and Screaming into the woods!!

Right???

So, why do I even bring up this taboo subject?

What if I told you bankruptcy is only a taboo subject amongst the poor, and in fact, most bankruptcies are filed by the rich and wealthy?

What if I told you in some circumstances, filing bankruptcy can make your credit score go up?

What if I told you about my experience with filing bankruptcy while my credit was at 580, and within 5 years, my credit score was rebuilt to 750? This was long before I truly knew anything about credit.

What you'll find as you research bankruptcy is there are many factors that could make this extremely bad option turn into the absolute best thing that ever happened to you!

If you can no longer afford to pay your large debts, have failed to negotiate with your creditors successfully, are facing foreclosure, receiving dunning notices from lenders, or getting summons for court appearances to defend yourself from wage garnishments and repossessions, filing for bankruptcy may be an option for you to explore.

Filing bankruptcy can help you eliminate certain types of debts or create a repayment plan for other debts. It will also halt collection efforts, stop lawsuits and possibly save your home. However, it has some negative consequences, relating to the credit profile, which makes future credit approvals slim to none.

Having a bankruptcy on your credit profile is usually a red flag for lenders, and makes it much more difficult to get loans, and leads to lower ratings and higher interest rates for whatever you choose to apply for, including insurance.

Although filing bankruptcy is usually associated with a horrible affect on credit scores, data shows that most bankruptcy filers will see a rise in their credit scores within two years of the filing date.[5] If the court discharges the debts, the proper rebuild methods will cause the credit scores to bounce back in an efficient manner.

If your situation necessitates filing for bankruptcy, you would start the process by filing a petition with the bankruptcy court after completing a credit counseling session and receiving a certificate of participation. The counselor assesses your situation, looks into alternatives to bankruptcy, and offers debt management advice. Depending on the circumstances of your case, you can file for Chapter 7 or Chapter 13.

Most people file for Chapter 7 bankruptcy, which requires a federal court-appointed trustee to sell off a few assets (if applicable) and utilize the funds to partially repay the creditors. Following this liquidation, your debts are erased or discharged.

When filing for bankruptcy, work with a reputable bankruptcy attorney to retain the assets you want to keep, such as your car, work equipment, household items, and any equity in your home.[6]

With Chapter 13 bankruptcy, it does not require liquidating your assets. Instead, the court approves a manageable repayment plan for all or a portion of your debts over three to five years. In addition, the court has the authority to discharge some of your debts. This is usually the best option if you own a home or other valuable assets that you want to keep while making the agreed-upon payments.[6]

Once you decide to file, the bankruptcy case will be heard in a federal courtroom.

Because of the legal and financial consequences of filing for bankruptcy, it's essential to consult with a qualified lawyer or attorney. You may be eligible for free legal services if you cannot afford a professional. Make sure to explore all options before attempting to do all this yourself. The following are good places to start obtaining proper legal counsel:

- Legal Services Corporation
- American Bar Association's Legal Help website

Chapter 7 bankruptcy remains on your credit report for ten years, while Chapter 13 stays on your record for seven years.

As you can see, there is a BDEP solution for everyone, and there is a method that will work for you to eliminate bad debts in a quick and effective manner.

Once you have the bad debt under control, you can focus on laying the foundation for the next 40+ years of your financial journey.

In the next chapter, you will learn about the "most obvious" retirement strategy that we're tricked into believing when we enter the workforce.

This "picture perfect" retirement program is an outline the government has convinced us to mindlessly pursue – and why, in today's modern times, the government's plan will, unfortunately, keep you moving backward away from retirement until it's too late!

～

KNOCK KNOCK KNOCK SOUNDS MY HAND AS I KNOCK ON THE METAL door to a dimly lit office.

No answer.

And it's dark.

This don't look like the place? Did I get the address wrong?

I double-check Google Maps. It says I have arrived.

The directions led me into an industrial area on the outskirts of San Jose. The drive was 20 minutes longer than expected, which is why I am 20 minutes late. As I pulled into the large parking lot, there were only one or two cars parked in front of an enormous office building. And the entire building looked dark.

I look at my phone's message again.

TIM: When you get here, come up to the 3rd Floor.

When I arrived I walked up to the front doors of the dark building, and tried to pull the one of the large glass doors open.

They were locked. So here I am knocking. At an empty, dark office building.

I try calling Tim once more. No answer. *Ok, now I'm really late!*

I contemplate leaving. It would be easy to just get in the truck and drive away. *But it was such a long drive!* This is the right place, according to Google. *Why isn't he answering?*

As I look around the base of the gigantic building, I notice a dark staircase that leads up to the third floor, along the side of a concrete wall. It seems like a long shot, but I quickly dart up the steps to see if anyone is there.

As I arrive at the top of the stairs, I notice a door ajar, and I step inside.

Once inside the door, I am standing inside a very large cubicle office space, with half the lights on, and half the lights off. A cleaning company is vacuuming around the office in various places. Two or three people are scattered around the cubicles within their cell, sitting in front of their desks, typing into a computer screen, working late. No one seems to notice my existence in the slightest.

This can't be it! I walk slowly around the office for a couple minutes, and then leave the same way I entered, finally convinced that I should leave this place and never return.

I call Tim again. Voicemail.

"This is dumb. I'm out," I say to myself as I descend the dark flight of stairs.

4

THE OLD LEGS

"The greatest of all mistakes is to do nothing because you think
you can only do a little."

—Zig Ziglar

I pull my keys out of my pocket as I get to the bottom of
the steps, and proceed to walk along a pathway lined
with dozens of trees and low bushes. While walking
along the curved pathway, it appears that one of the low
bushes is missing.

When I pass by the missing bush, I discover the dark pathway
splits in two, with a new path leading between the trees and
bushes. The newly discovered path looks inviting. I turn left,
and walk down the path. *I don't think this is it, but, O what the
heck?*

Quickly striking a few steps forward onto the new path reveals that this gargantuan triangular-shaped building has an entire other side (wholly hidden from where I was before). This side of the building has another vast parking lot (completely disconnected from the parking lot where I had parked).

As I walk closer to the detached parking lot, hundreds of lights come into view illuminating dozens and dozens of parked cars and trucks. When I turn the corner to walk around to the new entrance of this enormous office building, there is no more darkness. Windows are emitting lights from within each room of the building, the brightness is flooding abundantly into the dark of the night. This side looks like a completely different building.

My phone buzzes with a text from Tim.

TIM: I am outside.

I peer toward the entrance about ten paces away from me, and recognize the outline of one person standing in a black suit with a royal blue necktie. It is Tim.

～

WANDERING AROUND IN THE DARK, IN THIS TRUE STORY OF MY LIFE from many years ago, is a perfect analogy for how most of are with our financial life. Wandering in the dark...

And it's hard to blame ourselves!

We get little-to-no *formal* education about how to deal with finances. For example, in 37 states it is mandatory for high school students to take a driver's education course to graduate. However, financial literacy is only a high school requirement in 26 states.

How can this be? Aren't there more people using money everyday than using a vehicle everyday? One could argue that using money without formal education could be just as dangerous as operating a car without formal education.

To credit the policymakers, the interest in financial literacy has grown over the years, and the government is recognizing it. Consider the difference in the year 2000, where only three states had the financial literacy requirement! It is encouraging to see the development as many states are starting to adopt financial literacy standards as the years progress.

To be clear, formal education for financial literacy is not the answer to all money woes, similar to how Driver's Ed does not prevent all accidents. The formal education from a young age is only the beginning. It's just meant to lay the groundwork to increase likelihood of success in the future.

Unfortunately, some of the lessons we will learn today in formal financial literacy training will be completely obsolete within the next 20-30 years.

Take for example, the three-legged stool.

THE THREE-LEGGED STOOL

Remember the good ol' three-legged stool of retirement planning? It became a famous metaphor among financial planners around the 1950s. It described retirement planning as three stool legs representing the three familiar sources of retirement income.[1] The three sources are:

- Employee pension plans
- Personal savings

- Social Security benefits

Compare these sources to an actual three-legged stool. If one of the stool's legs is missing, it cannot stand on its own, it will topple over. Similarly, all three of these pieces are required to lay a lasting financial foundation for the golden years. However, none of the three legs are expected to provide a stable retirement income on their own.

Let's take a quick look at each of the legs of the three-legged stool for traditional retirement planning.

Employee Pension Plans

The first leg of the stool is Employee Pension Plans, also known as defined benefit plans. These pensions are retirement plans in which employers save, invest, and distribute money on their employees' behalf. When the employee retires, the company agrees to pay them a monthly check for the rest of their lives. The exact amount an individual would receive each month depends on factors such as how long they worked for the company, their position, etc.

Fun fact: The first company to offer corporate pension plans in the United States was the American Express Company in 1875.

For the American Express Company, the workers had to meet three critical milestones to qualify for the pension:

- Work at the company for 20 years
- Reach the ripe age of 60 years old
- Receive a retirement recommendation from a manager and get the request approved by the board of directors and a committee.

The workers who met these three requirements would receive half of their annual salary while in retirement, up to a maximum of **$500 per year!** (That was a *lot* of money back then!)

After American Express Company's example, several large corporations followed in their footsteps by offering pensions to their workers as well. Soon this became a common practice.

Personal Savings

The second leg of the stool is personal savings, or funds that you have personally saved for retirement. The funds could be saved in various savings accounts, such as a bank savings account, or accounts explicitly designed for retirement savings, such as Roth IRAs and 401(k)s. Most times, an individual has little savings in their bank account but will have a percentage of their paycheck automatically deposited into their workplace retirement account.

Workplace retirement accounts (also known as employer-sponsored plans) are generally provided via an employer. They include 401(k), 403(b), and thrift savings plans. Although these accounts are provided through an employer, the worker is responsible for contributing to their account.

Employees can also use individual retirement accounts, such as a traditional IRA or Roth IRA. Self-employed individual retirement accounts are also available. They include solo 401(k)s and SEP IRA.

Social Security Benefits

Social Security is the third and final leg of the old three-legged retirement planning stool. It is a government entitlement program that provides workers with a lifetime income once they reach the qualified age and tenure. Qualified workers are typically those who contribute to the program through FICA taxes throughout their careers.

Workers can start to collect their Social Security benefits from the ages of 62 to 70. The later you delay collecting Social Security benefits, the more you will receive each month. The amount an individual receives is determined by how much they contributed to the program during their working days, but there is usually a monthly cap that changes over time.

Does the "Old" 3-Legged Stool of Retirement Still Work?

Back in the 1950s, the three-legged stool for retirement planning was a brilliant idea that achieved remarkable success.[2] The retirees had well-funded retirements that were supported by a mix of public and private retirement income sources. Social Security benefits and employer pensions guaranteed monthly payments beginning at the age of retirement. When personal savings were added, retirees had adequate retirement security. Smooth sailing into the golden dawn!

What could possibly go wrong with this perfect picture?

It would be nice if we all had the blueprint to retirement that would stand the test of time and be exactly the same for each and every person. Sad to say, the Three-legged Stool has NOT withstood the test of time. It is grossly outdated.

In the 21st-century workplace, the three-legged stool approach to retirement planning has declined in effectiveness and accessibility over the last several decades. If you are early in your career, it is perfect timing for you to snap out of the trance of believing in this "smoke-and-mirrors" path to retirement.

Let's break down why each of these legs has already broken, and in fact this stool has already disintegrated.

Pensions Phased Out

Firstly, the traditional pension system has been completely phased out in most industries.[3] Most small employers do not provide pension plans, leaving the majority of workers with no recurring income at retirement age.

However, this is not only a small employers' problem. The majority of large companies no longer provide pension plans to their new employees either.

According to one study, only 16% of Fortune 500 companies provided pension plans to employees who started working in 2017 or later.[4] This was a significant decrease from 59% in 1998. Pension coverage seems to be attainable only for public sector employees, such as firefighters, teachers, and other government employees.[5]

The traditional pension plans have been gradually replaced by 401(k)s and other employer-sponsored plans, in which employers match an employee's contribution in full or part. However, the employer match doesn't offer nearly the same retirement security as a guaranteed pension.

With pension plans, workers are guaranteed monthly checks. On the other hand, 401(k) plans place many responsibilities squarely on the shoulders of the employee. Factors such as contribution levels, investment options, withdrawals, and tax consequences must be deeply considered by the employee. There are no guaranteed benefits in retirement with the 401(k) and other similar plans. In fact, if you leave the job too soon you may not even get access to the company match at all.

When you read into the details of these plans, you'll realize 401(k)s have more in common with a glorified savings account that has multiple strings attached.

So, should you rush to find a boss who will give you a pension?

Not so fast!

Let's be clear that a guaranteed pension can still come with risk. For example, when Bethlehem Steel declared bankruptcy in 2001, the US Pension Benefit Guaranty Corporation took over its pension plan. The outcome? Most of the company's employees saw their expected payments reduced and insurance and health benefits stripped away.[6]

This is where the other two legs of the stool are SUPPOSED to step up and take the slack.

Social Security Phasing Out

Another significant disruption that has arisen in the three-legged stool is the announcement that Social Security, established in 1935, will experience a reduction in benefits after 2034.[7]

Social Security benefits were a strong pillar of a solid retirement plan because of the guaranteed lifetime payments, no matter your employer. However, this pillar appears to be on the decline. So what's actually happening to Social Security, and is there a remedy?

As mentioned earlier, Social Security reserves are expected to be depleted starting in 2035. But before you can understand what's truly happening with this leg of the stool, you need to know how Social Security works.

Social Security is funded by payroll taxes deducted from employees' paychecks to fund payments for social security income. 85% of this money is used to pay current retirees' Social Security benefits, with the remaining 15% going to a trust fund that pays people with disabilities.

The worker-to-beneficiary ratio must always be at a healthy balance to keep the Social Security trust fund stable.

This is comparable to a pyramid structure. The bottom of the pyramid must be wide enough to support the weight of the top of the pyramid. If the top of the pyramid grows too wide, eventually the whole structure topples over.

In the early days, the ratio was fantastic since the number of current employees (workers) drastically outnumbered the retirees (beneficiaries), resulting in surplus reserves for the Social Security fund. Unfortunately, as the years went on, employees started retiring sooner, collecting social security benefits earlier, and living longer.

To compound this, baby boomers are the largest segment of the population. And since we will see 80-85% of all baby boomers retiring over the next 10 years, the social security reserves are expected to be exhausted by this time.

After 2034, retirees will vastly outnumber younger workers, making it nearly impossible for the program to keep up with the strain. This does not mean that Social Security benefits will be entirely eliminated. Instead, retirees will receive about 20% lower benefits than what they are currently receiving.[8]

Additional changes (such as later retirement age qualifications, higher interest rates, and further payment decreases) could occur before 2034 to keep the program stable. But we must admit that this is not the time to wait for the government to fix things in the hope these future changes will benefit you.

With unpredictable future payouts, Social Security is no longer reliable for today's modern generation.

As pensions become rare and Social Security payouts are reduced, workers are continually fed this promise of a retirement using the old three-legged stool, even though they are unwittingly banking on one leg, the employer savings accounts.

Employer savings accounts include 401(k) and other types of plans (also called deferred compensation plans). These accounts are now the primary source of retirement savings for most employees.

There are many, many, MANY reasons why it's not only foolish but outright fatal to use this vehicle as your sole source of retirement. However, we would need another 200 pages to debunk all of the myths. In this book, we shall reveal one tiny detail that most investors are unaware of in their 401(k) plans: hidden fees.

These fees are not hidden per se, as the U.S. Department of Labor requires the fees to be disclosed, but they are normally buried in the prospectus and jargon. If you went to look up your fees right now, you may not find them until tomorrow.

In 2011, AARP discovered that more than 70% of 401(k) participants were unaware they were paying any fees at all. As a result, the Department of Justice ordered 401(k) providers to disclose all costs associated with the plans.

These fees are eating away at your returns in the long run and this is another reason why employees using this account as their "retirement barometer" will end up working past their desired retirement age. Depending on the plan and your portfolio allocation, these fees could exceed $100,000.

There are two basic categories of 401(k) fees:

- 401(k) plan provider fees
- Investment management fees

401(k) Plan Provider Fees

The fees in this category are related to the day-to-day operation of the 401(k) plan. The fees cover:

- Record keeping services
- Trustee and custodial services
- Third-party administration services

401(k) plan provider fees are typically between 0.25-0.4% of your plan's total assets annually. Unfortunately, you can't do much about the plan provider fees.

Investment Management Fees

These fees are by far the most significant drain on your savings.

Each fund in which you invest has its own expense ratio (total fees in the form of an annualized percentage).

In general, actively managed funds have a higher expense ratio than passive funds. When making portfolio allocation decisions, you can consider the funds with a lower expense ratio if they fit into your investment goals and risk tolerance levels.

We are usually taught to focus on the overall return in the 401(k) investment, however to get to the bottom of how much these fees are costing you over the long run, you must crunch the numbers. You can use the FINRA fund analyzer tool or check each fund's prospectus to determine your funds' expense ratios.

Even though investment management fees are 1% on average (they typically range from 0.5 to 2.5%), and the costs may not appear to be significant at first, these small percentages will add up with time and compound interest.

Keep in mind that while 401(k) plans offer great benefits like an employer's match, this may dupe you into believing the account is not hemorrhaging funds while the fees continue to increase over time. The employer match helps to cover up the fees being paid into this program.

Also, remember, this third leg of the stool was never designed to be your only retirement income source.[9] This leg of the stool was supposed to be an "extra" account. Like a cherry on top. This is the reason why you cannot contribute that much money into these types of accounts. For example, in 2022, the maximum annual contribution allowed to a 401(k) for a single person was $20,500.

Such a level of savings is quite low for reaching a comfortable retirement.

Most workers in the U.S. live on more than $20,500 a year as a young person, so how would it be possible to survive on that as a retiree in the future?

Not to mention, inflation is still silently siphoning value away from your retirement savings. As the cost of living increases over the years, most people ignore it and don't factor it into their retirement roadmap. This is another reason why retirees who make a valiant effort to reach the "magic number" in their account STILL seem to struggle to make ends meet in their golden years.

It's like the finishing line keeps moving farther away the closer you get.

In the first book, *Personal Finance For Teens and College Students*, we did a deep deep dive into taxes, better known as the second "*money villain*". We will not go into much depth on taxes here, as it is covered at length in the first book. However, be mindful that once you finally access this supposed safe haven of money in the 401(k), you will come face-to-face with taxes. And you're not going to like it.

Read Chapter 2 of the first book for extensive detail on how this money villain specifically affects your retirement plan and how to access the remedies at your disposal.

Ted Benna, the inventor of the 401(k) plan, shares the benefits and drawbacks of 401(k) in his book "401(k)—Forty Years Later". His primary issue with the current 401(k) is the investment structure which he says he'd completely wipe away if it were up to him.[10]

According to Ted's documentation of the history of 401(k), the plan has changed a lot since its establishment, and *not* for the better. For example, when the 401(k) was first introduced, all fees were paid by employers, but now it's all on employees, which impacts the plan participants negatively.

In addition to the fees, the numerous investment fund options make the plan more complex. The 401(k) inventor begs us to realize that more is *not* always better, especially when experts in the financial industry are utilizing this product to create additional profits for themselves.

In the beginning, the original 401(k) plans had two investment options only. Today, the options are numerous and you are strongly recommended to consult a financial planner or advisor with 401(k) expertise to ensure you don't make poor choices in selecting your investment options.

We're Getting Too Darn Old For This...

Even if you find a lucky person who has successfully navigated these hurdles and achieved each pillar of the outdated three-legged stool for their retirement, you'll still have NO answer for another major issue... we are living too darn long!

The life expectancy keeps going up. In 1900, the life expectancy of an American newborn was approximately 47 years. Today, babies born in the USA can expect to live about 79 years. This is well over 50% *longer* lifespan! [11]

This is usually thought of as a good thing. We have sayings such as "Live long and prosper" and "Live a long, healthy life" which remind us of the idea that living for a long time is a blessing that many don't experience. And it is always viewed as a tragedy when someone we love "Died too young", regardless of the pop culture references which promote the "live fast, die young" theme.

Additionally, modern medicine and science continues making new discoveries each year which provide us with cleaner food, cleaner water, better air to breathe, and better medicines and therapies. We should be happy the life expectancy is increasing! That means these contributions to society have been doing a good job!

Unless you're referring to retirement...

In a recent study by Allianz, 63% of respondents said they would rather *die* than outlive their savings. This study shows it's not just the older generations that think this way, as 64% of Millenials surveyed also admitted they would rather *die* than outlive their savings.[12]

At the age of 62, when most people begin receiving Social Security benefits, the average woman has a life expectancy of 23.8 years, while a man has a life expectancy of 21.4 years.[13] In other words, you have a better chance of spending more time in retirement than you spent in college, high school, and prep school **combined**.

This is a *significant* amount of time that you must learn how to prepare for if you want a comfortable, stress-free retirement. For the ones who are lucky enough to live long, most will see themselves going back into the workforce, especially if they do not have a robust retirement package.[14]

THE NITTY-GRITTY

It's clear by now that the three-legged stool pillars are outside of your control. What's worse, the entities in control can change the rules at any moment. What if your employer suddenly reduces the 401(k) match or stops offering it altogether? What if the Social Security benefits are reduced earlier than expected?

One of the clear illustrations of this point is that the federal government has recently decided to redirect national 401(k) funds from your hard-earned retirement to fund the "country's needs". There has already been legislation passed in an attempt to enact these laws swiftly, without causing too much ruckus.[15]

With all that said, do you still think it's in your best interest to have a government-controlled retirement, or would you prefer the one that you have complete control over?

That's not a rhetorical question. It is a question you must answer for yourself.

If you're already nearing retirement, it's probably best to keep on with your current retirement plan if it's working. But for younger adults entering the workforce, you need a modern strategy that will set you apart and give you the confidence to make your retirement self-sufficient, allowing you to retire in any economic condition comfortably.

That's where the (NEW) three-legged stool comes in.

This modern, updated version of the three-legged stool is comprised of these pillars:

   i. Tax-Advantaged Accounts (TAACT)
  ii. Savings Bonds
 iii. Pension Creation

In the next chapter, we will dive into each of the new pillars in detail, beginning with TAACT.

~

"THIS IS MY GUEST, JULIAN!" TIM SPEAKS CONFIDENTLY TO THE FRONT desk attendant after we enter the large swinging glass doors of the office building.

"Hi, Julian! Sign in here please," the woman at the front desk gives me a clipboard to fill in my name, phone number, and other details. The guest list has over 100 names on it. "Here's your name badge, Julian," she says as she hands me a red sticky name tag.

"Ok, follow me this way," Tim leads me to the elevator behind the front desk as I apply the name badge to my white collared shirt. As we get on the elevator, Tim presses the '3' button, and the elevator carries us to the top floor of the building.

"Sorry I'm late. I couldn't find the place," I finally speak to Tim as the elevator slows to a stop and dings open.

"Oh, don't worry about it. I'm just glad you're here." Tim leads us out of the elevator down a long hallway.

"Is this where you have all your real estate meetings?" I ask Tim while following.

Tim doesn't respond. He continues walking.

All the doors we pass are closed, until he stops at one door that is cracked open. Suddenly, Tim slows down beside this door, crouches slightly lower, and peeks inside.

After staring inside for a few moments, he turns back to face me and says in a hushed voice, "Ok, you're going to be in here for this presentation, and I'll be back to get you once it's finished." Before my mind can process any thoughts, Tim opens the door and ushers me into this presentation room that is PACKED wall to wall in a cramped room with people listening to a man in a tan business suit speaking in front of a projector screen. A few people look back to catch who just walked in. With only a few seats available, I manage to walk across the laps of three people before snuggling into a metal chair. The temperature felt like it was cranked up by ten degrees in this windowless room.

I glance around me and cannot spot Tim amongst the sea of heads. *So he's gone again? Are these the people I'm supposed to meet? Are we all here for real estate?*

Once I settle in enough to pay attention to the speaker, I decipher that he is explaining a concept that he calls the "Rule of 72".

5

THREE WAYS TAXED

"The best time to set up a new discipline is when the idea is strong."

—Jim Rohn

This meeting is a little perplexing to me. So far, it sounds nothing like real estate.

Maybe it's coming later on in the presentation. I attempt to calm myself in the moment. *15 minutes, just give it 15 minutes.*

The tan-suited presenter is teaching about financial concepts. Since I had just graduated college months earlier, I assume the information would all be redundant and boring to me. After all, I had already passed a few college classes relating to finance.

After explaining the Rule of 72, the speaker reveals how taxes affect income. It is a very brief explanation, but eye-opening, as it demonstrates that if you double $1 twenty times, the resulting number is over $1,000,000 – but if you double $1, then tax it 25%, double that taxed number, then tax it 25% again, etc., etc., twenty consecutive times, the resulting number is only $70,000. I feel oddly stunned.

As I check my phone again, I realize 20 minutes have passed. *Okay, let's give it another 15 minutes. Just 15 more minutes. Tim still has to introduce me to his real estate people.* I hope the presentation will conclude soon.

After talking about taxes, the speaker describes how banks and insurance companies operate. Specifically how the banks need only 10% of cash on hand, and can lend up to 90% of their balance sheet (which equates to the banks regularly lending up to nine times the amount of money they have). While insurance companies are required to have 100% (or more) of their liabilities in capital reserves.

"In fact, the banks are actually insured by insurance companies," boomed the tan-suited man, as if he was giving a pregame speech. "Have any of you heard of FDIC?" A few hands raise in acknowledgment. "But do you know what it stands for?? It's the Federal Deposit *Insurance* Corporation!"

I've never heard of this stuff before! My mind wonders why none of this information was taught or retained from all my years of schooling. I sit up a bit in my seat.

Slide after slide after slide gets deeper and deeper into financial concepts that are entirely off my radar.

By the end of the presentation, I have completely forgotten that this was supposed to be a real estate meetup, as my mind is filled with the lessons I am learning here. I have learned more applicable financial concepts in one hour than I had learned from four years of University education.

∼

ONE OF MY BIGGEST TAKEAWAYS FROM THIS PRESENTATION WAS THAT no matter how much money you make, taxes can still wipe out a large portion of your income. Quickly.

The difference in long-term financial health is staggering when you compare someone who is knowledgable about how to reduce their tax burden, versus someone who has no idea how to reduce their tax burden.

When it comes to this subject, the age-old adage is highly accurate: "It's not about how much money you save. It's about how much you keep." Taxes are a significant issue that must be addressed.

In our first book, we dedicate multiple chapters focusing specifically on how taxes have earned the role of being our second "*money villain*" and how to minimize and eliminate the negative impact they have on you.

Although you cannot wholly eliminate taxes in retirement, you can set yourself up to stay ahead of the curve and reduce the tax burden in your golden years.

The first pillar of the NEW three-legged stool of retirement planning is to save your money in Tax-Advantaged Accounts (TAACT).

This is very important because if not planned carefully, taxes can cause shocks in retirement that eat away most of the growth in your savings. We'll crunch some numbers to demonstrate this later in the chapter.

While the impact of taxes may not always come as an unexpected surprise, it is still disheartening to part with a considerable chunk of what you worked so hard to save.

It's as though you have a silent partner (Uncle Sam) who's working with you behind the scenes of your working career.

It sure seems as though you're doing *all* the work — You have to build your resume, search for the right job, nail the interview, survive the office politics, drive to and from the job without getting into an accident for 20+ years, argue with your spouse and kids because you're feeling stressed out from the job (and have no one else to take it out on), get paid and realize it's not as much as you thought, then still figure out how to save some of this money for retirement... Just to name a few things on your list of to-dos (if you're self-employed, we can add a few more things to the list!).

While this is all going on, what's Uncle Sam's role in this partnership?

Kick back and collect a check!

What does Uncle Sam do with this check?

Whatever Uncle Sam wants! (Though lately this money has been devoted to military defense, social security, and medicare programs.[1])

Does this partnership sound fair to you?

Absolutely it makes sense to contribute your fair share, and give back to your family, your society, and your community.

However, when retirement arrives, you want to be able to live out your dreams in comfort, after all that hard work.

You don't want to be the elderly store clerk who has to keep working part-time jobs and move in with adult relatives because you had to give up one-third of your retirement savings to the government and can no longer afford the inflated living expenses.

What would you prefer instead?

What is your ideal retirement lifestyle in your golden years?

Take a moment to consider it.

Do you want a vacation kind of lifestyle filled with traveling the world and learning new cultures and customs?

Would you prefer to wake up in the same home for years, watching your grandkids grow up while hosting family taco night every Tuesday?

Do you want to own land, have cattle and a ranch, cultivate the soil, develop a garden, and have a self-sustaining environment?

Whatever your ideal retirement lifestyle looks like, achieving it requires you to begin proactive planning to make sure the dollars you put to work can extract your specific dreams into reality.

When considering all the factors of retirement planning, such as accumulating enough assets, inflation, recessions, ideal retirement age, retirement lifestyle, etc., there is one factor that should be near the top of the list, and that is effective tax planning.

The ultimate goal of tax planning is to reduce your tax burden in retirement, which will maximize your nest egg and allow you to keep more of the growth of your assets in the household rather than turning it over to Uncle Sam.

You can choose whether to pay your taxes now, later, or never. It all comes down to the type of account you choose. We're going to breakdown all three:

- Tax Now
- Tax Later (a.k.a. Tax-Deferred)
- Tax Never (a.k.a. Tax-Exempt)

You can use one, two, or all three of these strategies, but it's important to understand the benefits and drawbacks of each. This overview will help you better plan how various retirement income sources work together to ensure you don't run short or unnecessarily increase your tax bracket.

Tax Now

Tax Now means that the account doesn't provide any tax incentives for your funds. The gains in these accounts are taxed each year. These taxable accounts include checking and savings accounts, brokerage accounts, money market funds, etc.[2]

In taxable accounts, any increase in value or investment income (such as interest, dividends, capital gains, etc.) is taxed in the tax year in which it is earned. The tax rate for these accounts depends on how long you have held the investment.

The primary benefit of taxable accounts is that there are no annual limits or restrictions on contributions, withdrawals, or investment income. Since these accounts are not specifically designed for retirement, you can withdraw funds from them at any time without penalty or age restrictions.

Taxable accounts also allow you to have a joint owner on the account (which is not allowed with retirement accounts).

What is the best way to use Tax Now accounts to supplement retirement? Here are some of the best uses for Tax Now accounts:

- Savings that you may not need today and can sit on for a few years. This includes purposes such as emergency funds, a house down payment, car purchase, etc.
- Saving aggressively for retirement beyond what the contribution limits for tax-advantaged retirement accounts allow.
- Diversifying your portfolio to include investment options and strategies not available in tax-advantaged retirement accounts.
- Investment profits that you intend to use before reaching the age of 59 ½.
- No required minimum distributions (RMDs).

TAX LATER (A.K.A. TAX-DEFERRED)[3]

With Tax Later, you are able to defer taxes on income and investment returns, but you'll eventually pay them down the road, usually when making withdrawals. The investment vehicles that allow this tax strategy are also known as tax-deferred accounts.

Deposits for these accounts are typically deducted directly from your paycheck before any taxes are applied. This reduces your current annual taxable income, allows you to save pre-tax money, and allows your investments to grow for years without being taxed.

Deferring taxes as long as possible allows you to benefit from years or decades of compounding growth. Pre-tax income provides you with more funds to invest with today.

The most common examples of tax-deferred accounts in the United States are traditional IRAs, tax-deferred annuities, and employer-sponsored retirement accounts like 401(k) plans.

Remember, these accounts come with government-imposed contribution limits that vary yearly. There are also restrictions on withdrawals. You can only withdraw funds when you reach age 59½. Otherwise, you'll pay the tax, plus an additional 10% penalty.

Such rules and withdrawal limits are in place because breaking them defeats the purpose of the accounts, which is to encourage saving for retirement. Retirement, in this case, means beyond age 60.

Traditional IRAs also have RMDs, which are the minimum amounts you must withdraw from the account beginning at age 72.

This means, by the time you reach age 72, these accounts will not allow you to continue the investment without withdrawing and paying taxes, no matter if you don't need the money.

What is the best way to use Tax Later accounts to supplement retirement? Here are some of the best uses for Tax Later accounts:

- Income that you can set aside to invest for the next couple of decades.
- Take advantage of the employer match (if available) and receive twice as much money in your account by saving the percentage that will get 100% of the match.
- Diversify your retirement savings to include stocks, bonds, mutual funds, ETFs, and other creative investment products.
- Convert your tax-deferred account into a self-directed IRA to invest in physical assets, such as rental properties, precious metals, private equity, tax liens, and more.

Tax Never (a.k.a. Tax-Exempt)

Does a tax-exempt retirement sound too good to be true?

Never fear, for this is 100% real, you just need to know which accounts to use and how to use them.

The catch is, these accounts can only be funded with after-tax dollars.[4] As a result, your investment returns and withdrawals during retirement are entirely tax-free.

Tax Never accounts eliminate future taxes on your investment returns and distributions. This is especially helpful if you think taxes will be going up in the future. And if you look historically at income taxes over the past 100 years, you will find that we are currently in a period of very low income taxes compared to previous decades. So, if you had to guess, do you think taxes will be going up or down in the next 20+ years?

It's logical to think they will be going up!

Many retirees are also surprised by how their distributions from retirement accounts can accidentally push them into a higher tax bracket and potentially reduce their income when it's needed the most. Hence another reason why Tax Never accounts make so much sense.

The most well-known Tax Exempt accounts are Roth IRAs and Roth 401(k)s. The name Roth is derived from Delaware Senator William V. Roth[5], who advocated for tax-free investment accounts in the Taxpayer Relief Act of 1997.

Notably, a Roth IRA is exempt from RMDs.

Generally, these Tax Never accounts are the best for lowering your tax burden in retirement while also allowing your money to grow tax-free. The rules are simple. Invest after-tax dollars, grow them tax-free, then withdraw them tax-free in retirement. Who wouldn't want that?

What is the best way to use Tax Never accounts to supplement retirement? Here are some of the best uses for Tax Never accounts:

- Invest a consistent amount that you will only need after age 60.
- Take advantage of the employer match (if available) and receive twice as much by getting 100% of the match.
- Use the investment opportunities within these accounts, which include stocks, bonds, mutual funds, ETFs, and more.

- Save into a cash value life insurance policy in order to allow the savings to grow tax-free and be used tax-free when the policy is setup correctly and used properly.
- To simplify the process, simply purchase municipal bonds or specific notes issued by the federal government that will allow the investor to collect interest on the money without having to pay state and/or federal taxes.

To summarize, you will experience some taxes any time you receive money. The main distinctions between your retirement accounts are when the taxes are officially paid, the annual contribution limits in the specific accounts, the liquidity of access to the funds, and any age restrictions.

Tax-advantaged accounts include both Tax-Deferred and Tax-Exempt accounts. Although you will be required to pay taxes on the money in all of these accounts, the question of *WHEN?* determines how much tax you will pay versus the amount of your retirement savings you can utilize.

So, what's the right mix of accounts for you?

Fortunately, it is not a case of one versus the other. In retirement planning, you should strive for tax diversification. You've probably heard it said a hundred times that you should diversify your investment portfolio, and this also applies to tax structure.

First, we have yet to learn what changes in tax laws will occur in the coming years or decades. So, when you have multiple accounts with different tax rules, you give yourself more control over your tax bill(s) and more flexibility in withdrawing your retirement income. You can always monitor your taxable income, choose which accounts to tap into, and adjust your withdrawal strategy as needed.

Also, there is one approach that can be disastrous when all you want is relaxation and peace.

Disastrous!

This is the art known as "putting all your eggs in one basket".

For example, an investor only contributes to their 401(k) account every month and that's it. However, if something unexpected happens to that account, it takes your entire retirement with it. For example, if you end up in a higher tax bracket, you'll be stuck with a higher tax bill as a retiree.

The amounts you should save in each type of account will vary depending on factors such as your current tax rate, the desired flexibility when making withdrawals in retirement, lifestyle, retirement age, etc.

While Tax Now, Tax Later, and Tax Never accounts all serve different purposes, they can all work harmoniously to contribute to the success of your long-term money growth.

However, the true magic happens as you figure out how to utilize compound interest while avoiding taxes as much as possible.

Here's an example to illustrate how important taxes are in affecting your money-growing efforts.[6]

If you put $1 in an account and it doubled every year, you'd have $2 at the end of the first year, $4 at the end of the second year, $32 at the end of the fifth year, and so forth. By the end of year 20, you would have a grand total of $1,048,576.

One Dollar Doubled 20 Times
(NO TAX)

$1.00
$2.00
$4.00
$8.00
$16.00
$32.00
$64.00
$128.00
$256.00
$512.00
$1,024.00
$2,048.00
$4,096.00
$8,192.00
$16,384.00
$32,768.00
$65,536.00
$131,072.00
$262,144.00
$524,288.00

$1,048,576.00

It doesn't seem like $1 would grow to over $1,000,000 that quickly. Even if you look at the 15th doubling, it's only $32,768! The power of compounding really kicks in towards the end.

Now consider what would happen if the principal ($1) was invested in an account that was taxed every year.

This is the same dollar doubling every year, but each time, you pay tax at a 25% annual rate. You'll have $1.75 at the end of year one, 3.06 at the end of year two, $16.41 at the end of year five, and so forth.

By the end of year 20, you would have a paltry sum of just $72,570.64! That means you'll have paid about $976,005.36 in taxes compared to the first example.

Now Share With Uncle!

(25% TAX)

$1.00
$1.75
$3.06
$5.36
$9.38
$16.41
$28.72
$50.27
$87.96
$153.94
$269.39
$471.43
$825.01
$1,443.76
$2,526.58
$4,421.51
$7,737.64
$13,540.88
$23,696.54
$41,468.94

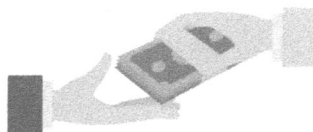

$72,570.64

Now you understand why the government imposes contribution limits and other limitations on Tax Later and Tax Never accounts. After all, who wouldn't want to put as much money as they can afford into these tax-advantaged accounts, especially if you can experience compound growth?

The government realizes this and wants to drain as much money as possible from your accounts into theirs.

This is why most people are just beginning to realize what "The IRS" acronym stands for. Do you know what the acronym stands for?

I'll give you a hint.

Your money is not yours...

It's THEIRS.

And many investors underestimate the effect of taxes and/or tax breaks on their income and savings.

It's easy to believe, "It's just $120 here, or $17 there, or 0.53 cents somewhere..." but when you factor in compound growth, we can truly see how we can have this work in our favor, or our detriment when it's working against us.

As another example, think about this from the perspective of a farmer.

A farmer must check the soil nutrients and adequately prepare the soil by tilling and adding manure. Later, they'll plant the seeds, water the plants, pull weeds, and keep an eye on the farm throughout the season.

After all of this, at the very end of the crop season, the farmer harvests their crops.

When do you think the farmer should pay taxes? On their entire crop after completing the harvest? Or how about on their seeds at the very beginning, before planting begins?

So how about you? Would you rather pay taxes on your financial harvest in your golden years or your seeds in the beginning? When do you think the tax collector would prefer to collect in this scenario? These are questions you must answer for yourself in regard to planning out your retirement savings.

And here's the good news!!!

You don't have to worry about the limitations associated with these tax-advantaged accounts. The more you learn about this, the more you'll understand that you can drastically reduce your tax burden in every account you own!

As an example, we have a little-known tax saving strategy, which can be structured for any person, any income, with just a checking account!

Get your free gift at 101MoneySecrets.com to learn more!

Now that you know how taxes work, in the next chapter we will explain the simple ways that income grows within an investment, how most people have been ill-informed when choosing how their money grows, and how you can get back on the right side of things.

~

By the end of the presentation, I am incredibly grateful to have received this introduction to the financial world in a brand new way.

The speaker ends the meeting saying they are looking for referrals to both learn the information and work in the company part-time. Although I am not interested to work with them (as the presentation slides had nothing to do with real estate), I know there are others who would benefit from the information.

As soon as the meeting ends, Tim appears in the hallway to greet me as I exit.

"Hey Julian, I want to introduce you to someone," he says.

Are these the people I came to see? I feel a sense of relief as Tim leads me further down the hallway.

"Sorry I missed you at the beginning! It was kinda crazy in here," says Tim.

"Yes, it was hard to find," I admit again. "Like, I was at an whole other building for 20 minutes."

"Haha, yea my bad bro. But hey, I want you to meet Mac," Tim finally arrives at the last office in the hallway. He knocks on the office door lightly, then opens it and proceeds to walk in. I follow behind him.

"...so did you understand what they were explaining in there?" a conversation is already happening inside of the office.

"This is Julian. He is my other guest tonight," Tim announces.

"Hey, what's up Julian!" conversation pauses for a moment as the tan-suited man from the presentation is seated behind a large wood grain desk.

"Just grab a seat," Tim gestures to a chair in the far corner of the office.

So is THIS the real estate meeting I've been thinking about this whole time?

"Did they teach you guys any of this stuff at LegalShield?" the tan-suited man behind the desk picks back up the conversation with the person who was already seated across from him, apparently Tim's *other* guest.

I wanted to reach over to Tim (who was now the entire length of the room away from me) and finally ask him about the people he wants me to meet. Wasn't that the reason for me being here tonight?

"No, they don't teach any of this, but it was great information!" The LegalShield man responds. "I think it would be smart to partner up with Tim and share the customers we have."

Partner up with Tim? I am finally beginning to connect the dots.

"That's a great idea. You guys should definitely partner," the suited man behind the desk continues. "This office did over nine figures in business last year, and Tim is one of our rising up-and-comers."

I look over at Tim, two seats away from me, whose eyes are twinkling.

"By the way, who are those people you have in mind that could use the info?" Mac asks.

"I'll have to look them up on my phone," LegalShield responds. "Can I share them with Tim later on?"

"Sure..." Mac starts.

"Sorry Mac, I have to step out for two minutes. I'm sorry," Legalshield gets out of his chair, and abruptly leaves the room.

"Let me go check on him," Tim says hurriedly as he shuffles out of the office.

Finally, the tan-suited man grudgingly pulls his eyes away from the office doors, which closed behind his two promising prospects. His eyes turn to me. "Oh, you're still here?!" says his face, while his mouth says, "Hey, what's up man? You're Julian, right?" with his eyes darting to the pad and yellow paper on his mahogany desk. "What did you think about the presentation tonight?"

"You shared a lot of good information. I wish they taught this in school," I blurt.

"That's what we're trying to do is share this with as many people as possible," I watch as he writes the name JULIEN at the top of his yellow pad.

"So, do you guys do any real estate here?" I inquire.

"No, not anymore. We used to," Mac looks up at me over his blue-framed glasses. "Did Tim tell you what we do?"

"No," I admit, sitting up in my seat. "I thought Tim was in real estate, but I didn't make it here tonight until the presentation had already started."

"Yeah, so when I first started, we were doing mortgages and refinancing," Mac informs. "But after the bubble popped, we focused more on investments and retirement planning." His explanation complemented by a two-finger gesture with his right arm outstretched. "Does that make sense?"

"Yes," I say instinctively, without fully processing.

Ping goes the phone in my pocket.

I place my phone in my lap to silence while reading the message I had just received.

TIM: I gave my friend a ride here tonight. Taking him back home now. Let's talk tomorrow.

!?!?@$%^#! went my brain.

I feel like jumping out of the top floor office window onto the roof of Tim's car at that moment (if only I had the confidence to stick the precise landing).

This is the bait-and-switch that I am not expecting. It is at this moment I finally accept that there are no real estate people I am here to meet. This meeting had nothing to do with real estate. And the people I am "meeting" had no idea I would even be here.

I look up from my phone, pretending to listen.

6

THREE GROWTH METHODS

"Change is the end result of all true learning."

—Leo Buscaglia

"Who is one person you think would benefit from this information?" Mac presses.

My frustration bubbles over, "There's so many people. But I gotta go man, it's getting late for me. I wasn't expecting this."

"You know you get $100 for every referral," Mac pipes back. "So you could make some money before you go. How many referrals you got?"

I could use $100 dollars. "So if I give you one referral, you'll give me $100?" I ask.

"Yeah!" Mac's voice inflection raises. "We gotta call them first. Not paying you for fake numbers." Mac pulls a wad of $100 bills out of his coat pocket, slips out one of the bills and slams it on the table. "Let's call them right now! Who you got?"

Huh? Right now?! Well... this still seems too easy. "Ok. Just one person. My uncle. He'll answer the phone. Here's his number—"

"No, you call them on your phone," Mac injects. "After you say hello, pass the phone to me."

This is getting weird. "Fine, whatever." *Here goes nothing.*

Ring Ring went the tone as I put the phone on speaker for Mac to hear.

"Hello?" answers a deep voice on the line.

"Hey, Uncle Bob," I realize I don't really know what to say.

"How's it going Julian?" Uncle Bob says to me.

"It's going well. Ummm... can I introduce you to someone?" I stammer.

"Introduce me to who?" Uncle asks.

Mac begins gesturing for me to give the phone to him. I pass Mac the phone.

"Hey Uncle Bob, this is Mac. How you doing tonight?" Mac says.

"Umm...Hi...Hey, I'm fine. Who is this?" Uncle Bob grunts.

"This is Mac, you don't know me but we both know Julian. He says you are one of his favorite uncles, and you two have a long history together."

"Uhh..yeah, that's my nephew."

"Well, Julian's here in my office right now. We're a financial company spreading financial literacy. Julian wants to get started with us on a probationary period, and we want to know if you wouldn't mind us coming over for about 20-30 minutes to hear what it is we do, and this would really help Julian with his training."

"Uhh..okay...I have to come where?"

"We will come to your house, it's not a problem, Bob. Does tomorrow or the next day work better for you?"

I could feel myself begin to sweat a little. *Wait, is this Mac guy really about to set an appointment? And do I have to be there? What about Tim?*

"Ok, tomorrow is not good, can we do the day after, I'll be free in the afternoon around one." As Uncle Bob gives this response, my jaw almost drops to the floor.

"Perfect, thank you Bob! We really appreciate it. Julian is here grinning from ear-to-ear. I look forward to meeting you in person."

Click Mac presses the button to hang up as he hands me back the phone.

What just happened?!? I try to close my mouth.

"Oh yeah, I forgot to mention..." Mac says as he tucks the loose $100 bill back into his coat pocket. "Before I can give you the $100, we have to go on this appointment together..."

∾

DURING THESE TIMES, I USED TO BELIEVE MY MONEY ISSUES COULD BE solved simply by making more money. I was easily allured by the promise of new money coming in.

And if the new money could be achieved with little-to-no effort (or intense effort for just a short amount of time), then I was all for it.

However, there was an issue that I faced which was what to do *after* the money was achieved. Years of money retention was wasted due to what I did with money after the money was received. I did not always put my money in the right places.

After I made money and paid off debts, fixed up my truck, and saved chunks of money into a savings account or CD, I would find myself needing more money within the next few months. There would be a new bill, new debt to payoff, and new things to improve with the truck.

How come I kept finding myself in this situation?

One major reason was most likely my money mindset. This can also be referred to as a "money thermostat". No matter how much money I received, my money thermostat would always cool or warm up to where I was comfortable.

If I had a large money deficit in my life, I would discover random opportunities, or find myself in situations where I would earn money in unique and miraculous ways. On the flip side, if I had a large surplus of cash, I would stumble upon unique opportunities to squander and get overcharged or duped out of all my savings and surplus capital.

As I grew wiser in the money game, I first had to adjust my money mindset and develop a knowingness that "part of all I earn is mine to keep". Then, after installing that in my brain, I next had to figure out where to keep this money to allow it to flourish in a diversified manner.

It would be so easy if saving and investing were as simple as putting money into one product and getting the best returns every year. I misled myself for many years, believing this was the road to investing, until I finally figured out it doesn't exist.

Usually, companies will promise great rates of returns which makes it seem as though your accounts will grow to astronomical levels. You won't find out the truth of the matter until you use the product to the maximum limits allowable, and discover the dividends aren't very astronomical at all. At that point, good luck trying to find any resolution from customer service agents or the booklets of terms and conditions.

To combat this, it helps to understand how your money grows within an investment to adjust your return expectations and strategize accordingly. Understanding the truth about how your money grows will keep you from succumbing to deals that sound very appealing at the outset, but end up costing more over the long run.

By the end of this chapter, you'll have a solid structure in place for maximizing the specific products you have and getting the most out of your returns.

Remember the lessons from the first book! Understand if you don't know the rules to the game there is no way you can win. It makes no difference if we're playing checkers, freeze tag, uno, dance dance revolution, or the money game, you can only win once you know the rules to the game.

One of the crucial keys to the game is to know how money

grows in your accounts. Generally, there are three ways money can grow in your account:

- Fixed
- Variable
- Indexed

These three ways also represent how interest rates affect your investments. Through this, you will know how your money is expected to accrue interest and shift over time.

Once you understand how interest rates affect your accounts, you can strategize to get the most bang for your buck, manage your expectations of the total value of the investment at the end of a certain period, and diversify your portfolio accordingly. Let's start with the first one.

FIXED GROWTH

When you put your funds in an account or security that guarantees a specific rate of return that remains constant, you have found a fixed account. In other words, the interest rate remains constant throughout the lifetime of an investment, whether it's 6 months or 30 years.[1] This makes fixed interest rates easy to understand and calculate.

For example, let's say you put $10,000 into an investment instrument with an annual rate of return of 5%. This means that you are guaranteed a 5% return on your money, regardless of how the market is performing.

At the end of the first year, your investment will earn a total interest of $500.

With a fixed interest rate, it's easy to calculate and predict the total interest you can expect over the lifetime of the investment.

The most common fixed accounts are savings accounts, government and corporate bonds, and certificates of deposit (CDs). There are also several exchange-traded funds (ETFs) and mutual funds that promised fixed returns as well.

VARIABLE GROWTH

Variable accounts provide interest rates that can rise or fall over the course of the investment.[2] Because variable interest rates are unpredictable, it is difficult to calculate the total interest to expect over time, unlike the fixed accounts.

As a result, investment vehicles with a variable growth structure are geared toward those who have a higher tolerance for risk.

What causes the fluctuations in variable accounts?

The interest rates of a particular asset fluctuate based on criteria set by the issuer. For instance, the requirements could be market conditions.

The most common variable interest rates come from securities, such as stocks. Generally, investing in securities means your return is linked to market rates. When the market trends higher, your potential returns grow higher, and vice versa.

INDEXED GROWTH

Indexed accounts provide a combination of features from the fixed and variable benefits mentioned earlier.

The performance and growth of an indexed product is linked to a market security or index, such as the S&P 500 or the Dow Jones Industrial Average. In other words, the rate of return will rely heavily on the performance of the linked index.

When the market rises, the potential return on this investment rises, and when the market falls, the return falls as well. However, the good thing here is that indexed investments provide a guaranteed base return, or a guaranteed interest rate, which is the lowest rate you're promised to receive, regardless of how far the market falls.[3]

So, within indexed accounts, you find both fixed and variable aspects. You have the guarantee of a base return, the same as you find in fixed accounts, and you also have the ability to participate in the upside of market returns, similar to variable accounts.

UPSIDES AND DOWNSIDES

So far, you have picked a winner among the three money-growing structures. However, remember diversification is required in all aspects of investing. Keeping all of your money in one growth structure is not necessarily the best practice because each has benefits and drawbacks.

Fixed Accounts provide stable returns and predictable interest rates over the asset's lifetime. They also include capital security and protection against market risks. With these Tax Now accounts, there are usually no limits to how much money you can invest in these products.

On the downside, the fixed growth structure is susceptible to interest rate risk and inflationary risk. Fixed rates are typically lower than inflation, meaning your money won't grow much and may lose value over the years. For instance, if the fixed rate is 3% annually and inflation rises by 4.5% over the year, your account would actually lose 1.5% in real value.

There is also something known as *Interest Rate Risk*, meaning that if the market interest rates rise above the fixed rate, you will be tied to low returns if no adjustments are made.

For Tax Later accounts, the major upside is that you can make a lot of money when the markets are moving upwards (and downwards, if you have the right knowledge). However, if the market turns against you, you could lose a lot of money in potential returns, and it could take years to earn back your losses. Unfortunately, faced with this circumstance, many investors find themselves forced to sell their investments at massive losses.

In Indexed Accounts, the interest rates you will receive depend on how the linked index or market performs. When the markets are doing well, you will make good returns. Unfortunately, you are likely to experience caps. This can be a cap on how much money you can invest into the product, and/or a cap on returns when the markets are doing phenomenal. On the flip side, when there is a market crash, you will have a floor that protects the investment from downside risk or negative returns. Even if the linked index keeps dropping for months, you won't earn a lower interest rate than the floor rate.

As an extra precaution, there are normally more fees associated with indexed accounts, depending on where and how you get involved. There are normally management fees associated with these products, but you may also find service fees, advisor fees, accounting fees, and many other fees, so bear this in mind when conducting your research.

For these reasons, all three growth structures are considered essential components of a well-balanced investment portfolio. Knowing how your money grows within an investment allows you to know how, where, and when the investment product would fit in your life as you progress toward the perfect investment portfolio for you.

Congratulations, you now know all about the first pillar of the modern three-legged stool of retirement, and how to involve TAACT (Tax-Advantaged Accounts) into your retirement portfolio.

In the next chapter, we will explain the second leg of the NEW Three-Legged Stool. We will demystify the confusion surrounding a certain well-known investment product and bring the clarity you've been searching for.

Grab a new sheet of paper to take notes, warm yourself a cup of tea, and get ready for this new adventure into your financial independence!

∾

PING GOES MY SLIDE PHONE, AS THE SCREEN LIGHTS UP.

UNCLE BOB: What was that all about? Call me.

What was that all about? Shoot, I wish I knew what this is all about!

As I drive my truck back up the I-880 freeway, my mind races with a million thoughts. Uncle Bob's text only compounds the situation. The hundred dollars doesn't seem worth it to me anymore. Plus, Mac never said anything about having to go on an appointment until after the appointment was set up.

I try calling Tim again. Voicemail. *Why this man not answering?*

This feels like too many confusing things happening at once for me. I decide to call Mac and shut this whole thing down. It's only been 15 minutes since I've left his office, and I've already had enough.

I call Mac and put the phone on speaker while I continue to navigate the highway.

"Hey, what's up Julian!" Mac answers the phone buoyantly.

"Hey Mac, this is too much for me. I don't think I can do this. Let's just cancel the appointment," I say, speaking a bit louder so he can hear me over the road.

"How come? What happened?" Mac asks.

"I just don't want to."

"Did you forget what you learned here tonight?"

"No, I didn't forget," I respond while going around a bend. "I agreed to give a referral to get a hundred bucks, but now it seems like I'm in the company. I never agreed to go on any appointments."

"All right, that's fair," Mac admits. "It's cool man, we don't have to go to the appointment."

"Ok great, you can just go without me," I am about to hang up the phone.

"No, I can't go either, Julian. You'd have to be there for this appointment to stick," Mac lowers his voice. "It's my fault. I thought like Tim said, you were here to partner with us to share the information—"

"I can't even get ahold of Tim," I interject.

"You know, it's just one appointment," Mac reminds me.

"Yea, I can't."

"Well, what if—" Mac starts as I hang up the phone.

I drive the rest of the way home slowly, silently mulling over everything that happened that night.

As I arrive at the frat house, my phone buzzes with a call from Uncle Bob.

I answer, "Hey Uncle Bob."

"Well, Hello?" He responds.

"Sorry about that call earlier," I begin. "I was at this money thing, and that guy was giving a presentation. I had referred you."

"Referred to me to what?" He asks.

"It was like, financial literacy. Different lessons on money subjects."

"Money subjects like what?"

"Uhh... well I don't remember everything," I confess. "But there was one thing, like... have you ever heard of the Rule.. of 300?"

"No," Uncle Bob now sounds interested, as I'm trying to figure out how to tell him it's okay to cancel the meeting. "What was that, the Rule of 300??"

"Umm, yea... Wait no, 32... I meant 32! Wait...." I chuckle softly at my predicament. "I don't think I can explain it. It was a lot of stuff."

"So you guys are coming by the house? Is it just you two?" Uncle Bob inquires.

"Did you still want us to come? I was thinking we could cancel if it's too much."

"No, you don't have to cancel," Uncle says assuredly. "If this is helping you out I'm fine with it, just wanted to make sure I wasn't getting tricked."

I laugh tenderly, "Ok Uncle Bob, we'll be there. I'll text you when we're on the way."

"Sounds good. I want you guys to teach me *all* about that Rule of 300..."

7

THE BORING INVESTMENT

"Faced with what is right, to leave it undone shows a lack of courage."

—Confucius

*K*nock Knock Knock*

Mac's hand curls into a fist as he lightly raps on the wooden dinner table from my childhood.

"So, knock on wood, let's say you were to pass away right now… What happens after that? Now that you're *dead*, what is set up for the family?"

"Umm..I have to check…but it's probably not much of anything," Uncle Bob is seated across the dining room table from Mr. Mac and myself, with a dejected look on his face.

The appointment has lasted much longer than anticipated, and uncovered much more than I was mentally prepared to accept. Not only had my Uncle Bob not heard of any of the financial literacy concepts, he was struggling to keep things afloat financially in his life.

"So what about this house we're in now? What's going to happen to it?" Mac inquires.

"I don't know," Uncle Bob says softly, eyes lowered, looking at the table.

"Is this something you want to take care of today?" Mac asks.

"I have to talk to my wife and see what we want to do," Referring to my aunt, who is surprisingly not here.

"So just to be clear... you don't have any retirement set up for yourself currently, and when you die, there's nothing set up to take care of the family. You see why we need to get this started, right?"

My uncle mumbles something unintelligible and nods meagerly.

This feels cringeworthy, and I am ready to end the meeting and leave immediately.

Not Mac. He's in his element.

"Thanks for your time, Uncle Bob. I know this can be a difficult conversation when it's your first time having it," Mac attempts to lighten the mood. "I truly appreciate your time, and last thing before we go... Julian came into the office yesterday and liked the presentation so much that he decided to refer you."

That is different from how it happened, Mac. This was all for $100, remember?

"Well, ok… I'm glad he did," Uncle Bob says while looking in my direction. "This gives me some things to think about."

"Now I know you're not ready to change your situation today, and that's fine because this is mainly for Julian's training, when he starts doing these appointments himself," Mac says with a smile.

By myself? I don't know whether to indulge in a fake smile, burst with a sarcastic laugh, or shoot Mac an intense glare for each new commitment he's placing on my shoulders. I hold my breath and stare blankly.

"So Uncle Bob," Mac continues. "Who do you know that would benefit from this information? Who do you know that you could refer to Julian, so we can share this with them and continue Julian's training?"

One part of me can't believe Mac is still keeping up the act that I am in training. Another part of me was curious if the next appointment would go the same way.

"Uhh, I don't have anyone that comes to mind right now…I don't know," Uncle Bob says in his best sound of uncertainty.

What? No one comes to mind at all?

"Really, you don't know anyone?" Mac speaks my thoughts out loud.

"I just need to think about it," Uncle Bob reiterates. "Can I give you someone later?"

After a few more softball attempts, Mac concedes that Uncle Bob isn't going to take action on anything at this time. We bid farewell, and Uncle Bob escorts us out of the front door.

"Make sure you let us know when you're ready to get started!" Mac says as we exit the house.

"All right.. You gentlemen enjoy your day," Uncle Bob replies while closing the door.

Turned down cold! Mac and I descend the porch steps and walk back to my truck in a somber mood.

~

NEVER EXPECTING TO GET LICENSED AND SELL PRODUCTS MYSELF, THIS appointment, which I had set up just to "make $100", turned out to be a big eye-opener to the lack of financial literacy in my family.

"Don't Be An Uncle Bob"

Share This Book
With Someone You Love

I learned that the elders in my family, much older and wiser than I, knew just as much about managing finances as me. Which wasn't much.

Of course, there was the idea of "save into the 401k", or "collect social security when you retire", and other outdated ideas. But in general, there was a lack of knowledge about basic financial concepts on issues such as taxes, interest rates, and investment strategies.

In our first book, *Personal Finance For Teens and College Students*, we introduce the GA Money System, which unveils a holistic approach to defeating the three money villains: mindless debt, taxes, and inflation.

One important aspect of the GA Money System is that money flowing through the system gets the best results when using safe investment instruments with predictable, secure returns.

For example, rather than investing in stocks as a value investor, choose to invest in a stock that provides dividends or income; or even better than stocks, invest in an ETF.

Whatever the instrument is, make sure that it can provide stable, consistent returns in all market conditions.

How do you determine if the returns from a particular investment will actually benefit you over the long run? After all, the purpose behind investing is to grow your money and prevent your retirement accounts from losing purchasing power in retirement – when you need it the most.

Keep in mind, crunching the numbers for long-term investments is not always easy, especially when compound interest is involved. But luckily, there is a simple formula you can use whenever you are about to make a decision about your investment options; this aforementioned formula is called the "Rule of 72".

THE RULE OF 72

The Rule of 72 is a simple mathematical formula for estimating how long it will take to double the value of your investment at any compound interest rate.[1]

The formula is incredibly simple. All you need to do is to divide 72 by the annual rate of return on the investment.

- Time period for investment to double (in years) => 72/Annual interest rate

Example: Assume you put $5,000 in a mutual fund offering a 10% annual rate of return, compounded yearly. Plug in the Rule of 72:

- Time period for investment to double (in years) => 72/10 => 7.2 years

It would take approximately seven years at a 10% annual rate of return for your investment to double in value. That means your initial investment of $5,000 will be roughly $10,000 in seven years.

This formula works well for an investment earning a fixed annual rate of return, which is compounded annually. Thus, it measures the impact of compound interest on your investment.

Compound interest is when the interest you earn on your principal balance is reinvested, and you earn more interest. This is a powerful investment concept that accelerates the growth of your invested money.

It's no wonder Albert Einstein once said, "Compound interest is the eighth wonder of the world. He who understands it, earns it; he who doesn't, pays it."

Let's briefly demonstrate the power of compound interest here:

Suppose you invest $1,000, and it earns 5% interest, compounded yearly.

You'll have $1,050 at the end of the first year ($1,000 + 5% of $1,000) and $1,102.50 ($1,000 + 5% of $1,050) at the end of the second year.

This means that during the second year, you earned the 5% interest on the initial deposit of $1000 PLUS the first year's return ($50).

With compound interest, the growth cycle continues even if you make no further contributions to the investment. The interest earned each year is reinvested and added to the principal, so the total balance earns more interest the following year. This way, you'll gain far more than if the investment does not allow for compounding interest.

Without a doubt, the earlier you begin investing assets with compounding interest returns, the more time you have to make a profit.

As you can see, compound interest is difficult to calculate after the first few years because the interest earned increases every year. Using the same example above, interest would be $50 in the first year (5% of $1,000), $52.50 in the second year (5% of $1,050), $55.13 in the third year (5% of $1,102.50), etc.

Years	Future Value (5.00%)
Year 0	$1,000.00
Year 1	$1,050.00
Year 2	$1,102.50
Year 3	$1,157.63
Year 4	$1,215.51
Year 5	$1,276.28
Year 6	$1,340.10
Year 7	$1,407.10
Year 8	$1,477.46
Year 9	$1,551.33
Year 10	$1,628.89
Year 11	$1,710.34
Year 12	$1,795.86
Year 13	$1,885.65
Year 14	$1,979.93
Year 15	$2,078.93

The Rule of 72 cuts out all the math of how much interest you earn each year and simply calculates the amount of time it takes to double your investment. For this example: 72/5 = *14.4 years to double.*

Apply this formula to various investments to see the difference in how quickly they double in value. The sooner an investment doubles, the more interest it can earn over time. As a result, the Rule of 72 can be a helpful guide in selecting investment options.

Inflation vs. Rule of 72

Unfortunately, the Rule of 72 works against us daily due to inflation. Think of inflation as a silent thief. It sneaks up on us in the middle of the night, robbing our savings of purchasing power and catching us off guard.

In 2022, the inflation rate in the United States jumped to over 8%. Using the Rule of 72, we divide 72 by 8% to determine how long it takes for inflation to reduce the value of our money by half.

- Time period for inflation halving the dollar value => 72/8 => 9 years

It takes only about nine years for the money now available to lose half of its purchasing power. Using the earlier example, you can see that while your investment has doubled in value in just over seven years, inflation also cuts its purchasing power by half during the same period.

Luckily, there's a way to combat this problem, which brings us to the second pillar of our new three-legged stool.

This pillar is not sexy, glamourous, or thrilling.

The lack of appeal makes most of us falls asleep simply by the mentioning of this. They are a foundation of our economy, but will only get a two-second reference on financial news reports.

The best meme for this would be a wrinkled, white-bearded grandfather peering over his glasses, smiling ear-to-ear while watching two turtles race.

This second pillar, the sleeping giant in your modern three-legged stool are well-known as "Bonds and Treasuries".

To keep things simple, we'll refer to all of the products discussed in this chapter as ***Savings Bonds.***

A bond is a type of investment issued by institutions, such as corporations, governments, federal agencies, etc. When you buy a bond, you're lending money to the institution, which will pay you regular interest payments and repay the initial investment amount after a set period of time.

When investing in bonds, you'll encounter various terms specific to bonds. We'll look at the keywords you'll come across in this chapter:

- **Maturity Date:** The date when the bond issuer returns your initial deposit. Bond maturities are classified as short, medium, or long.
- **Face value (a.k.a. Par value):** This is the amount the bond will be worth when it matures.
- **Coupon:** The fixed interest rate the bond issuer pays to bondholders regularly until maturity.
- **Price:** When a bond is issued for trading in the market, it typically has two prices: bid and ask. The *bid* price is the highest price a buyer is willing to pay for a bond, whereas the *asking* price is the lowest price a seller is willing to offer.
- **Duration risk:** Bond prices move opposite to market interest rates. When interest rates rise, the bond's price falls. Thus, duration risk measures how interest rate fluctuations may affect the price of a bond over time.
- **Bond rating:** Credit rating agencies assign ratings to bonds and issuers based on their creditworthiness to help investors understand the risk of investing in a particular bond.

What you'll soon find out is that all Savings Bonds are not created equal and are typically grouped based on the organization issuing them. Therefore we have government bonds, corporate bonds, and treasury bonds as the various types.

Corporate Bonds

Individual companies issue corporate bonds to raise funds for their initiatives, for instance, expansion. The interest rates on corporate bonds can be fixed or variable, but the interest earned is taxable.

Corporate bonds often have higher interest rate returns than municipal and government bonds to offset the potential downside.

Another downside of corporate bonds is that they have a higher default risk meaning your initial investment is not guaranteed. The company may fail to pay your initial investment back on the maturity date in whole or in part due to the company's financial position.

Therefore, when purchasing corporate bonds, it is best to avoid companies that are not financially sound or have little-to-no financial history.

Credit agencies usually rate corporate and government bonds to help investors understand the quality of the bond and its default risk. The primary purpose of these ratings is to help you determine the likelihood of receiving your initial investment back after the agreed-upon period.

Generally, you'll see two categories of bond ratings:

Investment-grade (highly rated), and

High-yield (lower ratings and junk bonds)

Corporate bonds rated below "Investment-grade" have higher yields and higher default risk. They are called *junk bonds* because of the higher default risk, and the higher rates should not entice you if you have a low-risk tolerance.

Treasury Bonds

Treasury Bonds (T-bonds) are also known as government bonds. The U.S. Treasury Department issues them to fund various government activities or projects like the construction of highways.

Because the federal government backs them, T-Bonds are considered risk-free and a source of stable income (interest payments are made every six months). The U.S. government has never defaulted on this debt. That explains why most people nearing, or in, retirement invest in treasuries. However, the interest yields of U.S. government bonds are typically lower than those of corporate bonds.

Furthermore, not all Treasuries are created equal.[2] The U.S. Department of the Treasury offers several types of debt securities that differ in terms of the length of maturity.

- **Treasury bills (T-bills)** are short-term bonds with one year or less maturity dates. The longer the maturity date, the higher the interest offered. You will not get regular interest payments over the bond term with a T-bill. Instead, you'll receive the face value (par value) plus interest earned at maturity.
- **Treasury notes (T-notes)** usually have a maturity date between two and ten years. You'll receive interest

payments every six months until maturity with a T-note.

- **Treasury bonds** have a longer maturity of between 20 to 30 years. T-bonds pay regular interest twice yearly until maturity, when the par value is repaid to the investor.

Whether the treasury instrument is a bill, note, or bond, the interest earned on all is subject to federal taxation, but is exempt from state and local taxation.[3] Keep in mind, treasury bonds offer a fixed rate for the entire term. Regardless of the fluctuations in market interest rates, the bond rate will remain the same until bond maturity.

Besides the stable returns, another perk of government bonds is that they are guaranteed. In other words, you are assured that you'll receive your initial investment when the bond matures. Unless you sell your bond before it matures, in which case the initial investment is not guaranteed. Depending on the bond's price in the secondary market, you may receive a lower amount for the sale than you initially invested.

Municipal Bonds

Municipal bonds are issued by government entities like a state, town, county, or city to raise funds for public projects like roads, parks, schools, and hospitals. The best part about municipal bonds is that the interest earned is exempt from federal tax. They may also be exempt from state and local taxes if you reside in the state where the bond is offered.

Due to the Tax Never benefits, municipal bonds tend to offer lower rates of return than other types of bonds.

There are two main types of municipal bonds: General Obligation bonds and Revenue bonds.

- **General Obligation bonds (GO bonds)** allow local and state governments to raise capital for projects that may not generate revenue directly, for instance, public schools. Thus, they are not backed by any assets or projects' revenue. Instead, GO bonds are secured by the full faith and credit of the issuing municipality. In other words, GO bonds are guaranteed by the state or local government's ability to collect taxes to pay the bondholders.
- **Revenue bonds** are meant to raise money for income-generating public projects, for instance, the construction of highways. These bonds are not secured by the government's credit reputation and taxing power, but by the revenue from the specific project (i.e. highway tolls). Because these bonds rely on a project's income, they are considered higher risk than GO bonds, and pay higher interest. They typically have maturity dates of 20 to 30 years.

Generally, due to the tax benefits, capital preservation, and hedge against inflation, it makes sense to invest in Savings Bonds.

Rather than parking your money in checking or savings accounts offering less than 0.1% interest, consider saving into a bond. They will help your overall portfolio to keep up with inflation much better and avoid huge swings in the market.

As an older person nearing retirement, you'll want to adjust your investment strategy by investing more of your portfolio in Savings Bonds. The consistent interest payments can be a continuous stream of income when the employment paychecks cease.

Also, most bonds, especially government bonds, are considered risk-free, which is perfect for people who prefer their investment portfolio to be more conservative. An investment portfolio with a healthy dose of Savings Bonds will take less losses when the market takes a big dip.

Savings Bonds offer several things that really matter as you get older: capital preservation, a regular stream of income, and a hedge against inflation.

For younger people, it's common practice to have less money in bonds, compared to more aggressive investments.[4]

Although younger investors have the benefit of time to take more risks and recoup losses if things take a turn for the worse, it is still worthwhile to slowly grow a portfolio of Savings Bonds as the riskier investments start to pay off.

Keep in mind that these investments are liquid, so you can pull out the money when you need it in a pinch. If you have an ITIN or SSN and a US address, you can purchase savings bonds directly from the US Bureau of Fiscal Service.

To learn more, visit 101MoneySecrets.com for your exclusive bonuses.

If you don't know exactly which Savings Bonds to get for yourself, you can buy a package of bonds wrapped into one single investment, called a **bond fund**.

Think of bond funds as splitting your money between a basket of bonds all at once. These funds are invested in various bonds: Junk bonds, municipal bonds, corporate bonds, and/or treasuries. They may also include mutual funds and ETFs as well, allowing you to invest in a whole range of low-risk products at once.

Bond funds have low minimum deposits and often offer better interest rates than money market accounts and certificates of deposit. However, bond funds may also come with higher management fees and commissions as they employ professionals to manage them. The fund's returns may also fluctuate.

Remember that as a young person, now is not the time to go crazy over Savings Bonds. The only purpose here is to help your portfolio to better keep up with inflation over your lifetime.

For example, you may consider using bonds to store certain savings like your emergency fund, insurance deductible, or downpayment for a large purchase. This works well since bonds allow you to access the capital if you need it.

The critical thing to note is the bond's maturity, rating, and tax rules. You should also read the prospectus carefully to double check the bond issuer's track record.

CONGRATULATIONS

Now that you understand the way Savings Bonds work, you have the knowledge to solidify the second leg of your updated, modern three-legged stool.

In the next chapter, we will unveil the final pillar of the modern three-legged stool, which outlines how to use the money you receive to springboard yourself ahead financially and effectively keep all three money villains in check.

~

"BEFORE I FORGET, THIS IS FOR YOU," MAC SAYS AS HE SLIDES A CRISP $100 bill across the table.

"About time! Thank you," I say between bites, while reaching across the table and picking up the money with salty fingers.

Mac and I sit in a corner booth at In-N-Out, sharing burgers and fries before the drive back to the office, where I will drop him off.

"So now you know why I wanted you to be there, right?" Mac asks.

"Cause you wouldn't have got in the house if it wasn't for me," I answer cheerfully, while taking another bite of my burger.

"Right, there's no chance he was letting me in. Plus, you got to see it for yourself firsthand. Nobody knows this stuff!" Mac exclaims. "It's just basic information about money and saving, and everybody needs this."

"Yea that makes sense," I agree.

"And it's easy, right?" Mac continues, carefully dipping fries in his ketchup and tossing them into his mouth. Doing his best to avoid staining his tan business suit.

"No, I don't think it's easy. *You* just make it look easy!" I chuckle. "There's no way I can go into my uncle's house and start asking him about his financial situation. I don't even know how to begin or what questions to ask!"

"Don't worry, it's not that hard. You'll get it eventually," Mac assures, mouth full of food.

There you go again, roping me into this company! I feel the urge to nip this 'training' thing in the bud. "Mac, you know the only reason I came was for the hundred dollars, right? What's all this stuff about my training and all that?" I say while picking up my soda to take another sip.

Ping

My phone goes off with a text message. I take another bite of my burger and pull my phone from my pocket, while Mac stammers and coughs, thinking of a reply.

The text message is from my aunt. I furrow my eyebrows and read the entire message three times. I can't believe what I'm reading. *No, this can't be!! We were just there!*

"Mac!" I forget about everything we were just talking about before.

"What's going on?" Mac senses something is different.

"Uncle Bob just had a heart attack. He's in an ambulance right now."

"*What?!* You're kidding me," Mac drops his sandwich down on the table.

"They don't know if he's going to make it.." I feel delusional.

Mac and I stare at each other intensely for several seconds.

The news stops us both dead in our tracks.

8

PENSION CREATION

"You can't have the fruits without the roots.
It's the principle of sequencing:
Private victories precede public victories."

—Stephen Covey

Weren't we just with him?! We were just with him! We were just at his house...

My mind is on repeat as we traverse the hospital, looking for the waiting room we were given. Mac asked to join me, canceling his meetings for the rest of the day.

As we get off the elevator on the 13th floor, my hand starts trembling slightly. *Is this all my fault?* I consider that this is the first time I've seen Uncle Bob experience any health issues. He is only in his fifties!

We arrive to the waiting room. Only a few of my family members are there on this weekday afternoon. I lock eyes with my Aunt Rachel, Uncle Bob's wife. We give eachother a long embrace.

"How is everything going?" I ask.

"Your uncle just had heart surgery," Aunt Rachel responds in a saddened tone. "He's been stabilized but hasn't woke up yet. Do you want to see him?"

I nod yes. It doesn't make sense not to. Mac stays behind while I follow Aunt Rachel down the hall to the hospital wing of intensive care rooms. We walk in silence for about two minutes.

After reaching a particular spot, Aunt Rachel slows down to pause before a door. She turns around to face me, "Your uncle is in this room here," she says in a hushed voice. "He won't be awake for another couple hours, but I'm told he can hear everything happening around him." Aunt Rachel steps aside and ushers me to enter.

I enter the room to find Uncle Bob lying in a hospital bed, surrounded by medical devices and monitors. His heart rate is beeping at a steady rhythm. There is the *hiss* of a breathing machine that looks to be pumping air into his body. There are wires attached to various parts of his arms, and a long plastic tube coming out of his mouth. Uncle Bob's eyes have dark circles around them.

What did we do?! The guilt consumes me in the moment.

Sensing he can hear me, I summon the courage to blurt out the words, "You can't go out like this Uncle Bob. Everyone's gonna think this was my fault. I'mma need you to get well soon. And live another 10 years *minimum*."

❧

Most of us don't *want* to die, and we don't want anyone close to us to die either.

Unfortunately, avoiding or ignoring death is not the way to approach life. Death is guaranteed. Death has a 100% success rate for all men, women, and children born in human bodies. Even the bright-spirited people who live to be well over 100 years old eventually die.

This is a part of life that we learn to embrace in our own way as we come to learn as a society that it is much healthier to embrace death, because this allows us to be better prepared when that time comes. With better preparation, death won't have as large of a shock to the family. When it is embraced we can take this news in stride.

Of course, we generally prefer death to happen to a person after they have lived a nice, long life, well after retirement, and long into a person's golden years. However, when most people die, they rarely have prepared themselves adequately, and pass away with very little savings, no life insurance, and no wills or trusts.

There are many areas to discuss around the subject of death, but in this book we will concentrate on one area of your life that you can begin to build now, so that the transition to your golden years is smooth and financially satisfying.

By the way, do you know why retirement is referred to as "the golden years"?

Is there anything golden about retirement?

This is a serious question.

What makes it golden?

Why not call it the bronze years?

Silver years?

Or how about the Platinum years??

There is a story behind this about why it was chosen to be called the *Golden Years*.

Del Webb & The Sun City

Del Webb and his company coined the phrase "golden years" in 1959 when marketing their new project called the Sun City retirement community.

At the time, Americans feared retirement because it represented years of decline in every aspect: financial well-being, physical and mental health, learning capacity, etc. As a result, people were unwilling to plan for, let alone think about, the retirement days awaiting them at the end of their working years.

This made it difficult for the financial services industry to sell pensions to Americans. They had to find new ways of redefining retirement and the entire concept of aging, to sell pensions, annuities, and other retirement investment vehicles.

In 1952, many leaders in the financial services industry attended the National Industrial Conference Board meeting.

One of the day's speakers, the vice president of Mutual Life Insurance Co., urged the financial industry players to do a better job of spreading the concept that "old age can be beautiful and that the best life is yet to come." Webb and his team were the first to help realize the then-new concept a few years later through the Sun City retirement community marketing.

Webb's advertisements sold Americans a new, captivating, and fulfilling retirement dream. According to Webb, retirement would not be about helpless and miserable aging, but an endless vacation—an age of freedom from employment and mid-life responsibilities.

The picture-perfect scene they came up with for the "dream retirement" was a happy retiree sitting by the poolside sipping their favorite drink, or playing golf at any time of the day inside of a well-built retirement community.

However, Webb's executive team was skeptical that retirees would even consider such an idea, and they had reason to be. Every psychiatrist the executives consulted dismissed the project as *insane.*

Webb's Sun City was the first retirement community about to be created with a shopping center, golf course, and recreation center. Still, why would seniors abandon their current homes and families to live in post-retirement housing in 1960s Arizona?

And who would be willing to provide a 30-year mortgage to people in their 60s to afford the homes?

Surprisingly, upon campaign launch, people began to buy into Webb's "golden" retirement dream.[1]

About 100,000 seniors visited Webb's six retirement model homes during the week of the grand opening. It was a smashing success. Soon, more retirement communities sprung up, such as Leisure World, selling the idea of retirement as a time of pleasure.

Today, Del Webb has 55+ retirement communities that provide several post-retirement living options, activities, and experiences.

After the rebranding of retirement, people were no longer afraid of retirement and planning for it, which made it very easy for the pension industry to take advantage, as well as other competitive retirement planning products.

The Rise & Fall Of Employer Pensions

Even though employer pension plans, in general, were widely adopted in the 1950s, they are much older. In fact, American Express Company was the first employer to create the first private pension plan in 1875.

However, employer pensions gained much more traction after Webb's retirement revolution in the 1960s and reached their peak in the 1980s. In the 1980s, approximately 38% of private-sector employees had an employer-sponsored pension plan.

Most large corporations saw this as an opportunity. They used pension plans to attract and retain their best talent. And it worked to perfection. Employees increasingly started to work for the same company for decades. In exchange, they secured a retirement income that they couldn't outlive.

For those of you who are unfamiliar, employer pensions provide fixed monthly lifetime retirement benefits. The amount you receive each month as your benefit upon retirement is determined by how long you worked for the company and your average income during your employment days.

Plus, the longer you work for a company, the higher your monthly salary will likely be. Thus, our grandparents' retirement plan was to secure a good job as soon as possible after graduation, and work for the same company for 40 years.

Sounds like a great plan, doesn't it?

Unfortunately, this dream retirement plan is not a reality for most people in the newer generations.

We no longer work in the same company for 40 years.

In fact, according to the United States Bureau of Labor Statistics 2022 report, the average employee tenure is 4.1 years.[2]

Plus, even if we worked for the same company throughout our entire careers, most private employers no longer offer employer-sponsored pension plans.

Another challenge is the increasing life expectancy.

While it's wonderful that we have the potential to live longer lives, it comes with its own set of challenges. In the 1960s, the golden years began at 65 and lasted less than a decade, but today, they can now last two or more decades, which is double or *triple* the time.

With such changes and shifting economic conditions, the younger generations can no longer rely on employers to take care of their retirement. Most people are waking up to the idea that we need to find a new way to create a reliable and independent pension plan for ourselves.

Old-school parents used to believe their children could be their pension.

While I'm sure *you* wouldn't put that pressure on your child, parents relying on their children to take care of them as they age is a very common theme.

As long as you rely on external factors in retirement planning (for instance, family support, traditional investments like stocks, employer pensions, etc.), there will always be uncertainty about your financial future.

According to a recent Zety study, the fear of retirement triumphs over the fear of death and sickness in 40% of surveyed Americans.[3] Most of these anxieties stem from the fear of running out of money in retirement and losing employment-based healthcare benefits.

Financial stress is a major culprit for the unhappiness and misery among the retirees I have met. Lack of financial security often pushes some retirees back to the workforce to make ends meet.

Also, those in power can change the rules of the game for the worse at any time.

However, if you _build_ a pension, you will be more confident that your golden years will go smoothly, even if you retire at a younger age and live a long, long life.

With the information contained in this book, after you have implemented it in your life, you will not have a miserable retirement. Additionally, if you choose to continue working into your sixties, it won't be for financial security; it will be for your sanity, or the social network, or other non-financial reasons.

The first thing you must do to plan for retirement is to avoid the trap of relying on external factors, such as your boss, your children, or other family members.

Building Your Very Own Pension

If you are like most employees today, and you don't have the luxury of access to employer-sponsored pension, you can still obtain financial security in retirement by securing a private pension. Keep in mind when discussing private pensions in "the real world", most financial advisors will point you to guaranteed annuities.

An annuity is an insurance contract you enter with an insurance company to which you'll send a one-time lump sum or series of contributions over time. At retirement (or sooner), the money you put into an annuity is converted into regular income that can last the rest of your life.

You can start receiving the payments immediately or at a later date. Annuities that pay immediately after contribution are called Immediate Annuities or Single-Premium Immediate Annuities (SPIA). In contrast, those that pay out at a later predetermined date are known as Deferred Annuities.

People in or nearing retirement usually opt for the immediate annuities, while those with many more years to work prefer to go with deferred annuities.

You can choose the duration of your payment distributions, for instance, you can receive payments that only lasts for 20 years. Or you can also choose to receive payments that will last the rest of your life, if you don't want to accidentally outlive your payments.

One of the benefits of using annuities for retirement savings is the guarantee of capital safety and consistent income for the rest of your life, or a set amount of time. If you die before exhausting your disbursements, the payments will be paid to the beneficiary you designate.[4]

The downside of annuities is their illiquidity and lack of a huge capital appreciation. Early withdrawals are subject to rules and penalties. The payouts you'll receive are the initial investment amount and any gains, and you should expect fees and commissions from the insurance company, which can eat away at the gains. Also, unlike a 401(k), the funds you contribute to an annuity do not reduce your taxable income.

Remember, not all annuities are designed equally.

You will come across the following types of annuities that carry different levels of risk and payout potential:

- **Lifetime annuity:** You will receive regular payments for the rest of your life. The income you'll receive each month depends on the contract terms.
- **Fixed-term annuity:** This type of annuity will pay you an income for a set period starting from one to forty years. During your last payment (maturity), you'll receive the entire balance (principal plus investment growth, minus received payments).
- **Enhanced annuities:** These are designed for people with an illness or health condition like cancer, stroke, kidney failure, etc., that can potentially reduce life expectancy. Thus, it offers higher retirement income than other annuities.
- **Investment-linked annuities:** This is a lifetime annuity in which you choose what portion of

guaranteed income you desire, and the rest is linked to the performance of investments. If the markets do well, you can get a higher income; if the opposite happens, you are only promised the guaranteed amount.

Annuities are structured for stability in retirement income, especially for anyone who worries about outliving their retirement savings. Annuities are *not* meant for capital appreciation.

Your initial investment is guaranteed, giving investors peace of mind in retirement. This is a pension that you can create right now. However, living your dream life on today's average salary is almost impossible, let alone a *portion* of an average salary.

This will leave you afraid of running out of money during retirement (as most retirees do) since the rising costs of living and healthcare increases will outpace the income from company pensions. I'm sure you've heard stories of retirees who return to work for additional income or work part-time to make ends meet.

To combat this, you need to take the time to CREATE a personal pension that can pay you for life, whether you are working or can no longer work. The best way to do this is to start creating or acquiring an asset(s) that can give you a cash flow for life.

This concept is beyond the idea of simply "supplemental" income. It's about *passive* income, which can take care of you and your family once the employment income dwindles or ceases.

Passive income is the best path to retirement at any age.

It is an ongoing, steady income that requires minimal effort once you have made the initial investment of money, time, or other resources. In short, your money or initial effort will work for you without having to do anything—eventually eliminating the need for you to trade your time for money.

Some of the examples of passive income ideas include the following:

- Build up a $ 1 million investment into a quality dividend stock
- Build a monetized YouTube channel with evergreen content
- Purchase a portfolio of rental properties which a property manager maintains
- Write a book that generates consistent royalties
- Invent a successful product
- Build an affiliate website in an interesting niche
- Earn Music royalties
- Start a streaming service
- Own a portfolio of billboards that companies will pay you to place their advertisements on them.
- Start a podcast
- And much more...

Each of these passive income streams has its pros and cons. Some endeavors like acquiring a certain amount of dividend stocks may come with a bit of risk. While other endeavors have almost no risk at all, but require a large investment of time upfront.

Once a stream of passive income is created, it may or not be 100% passive. Some passive sources of income will require regular attention for 5-10 hours each week, while other sources of income will require only 5-10 hours of attention each *year*, or less!

The important thing to do is to realize that you are living in a time when you must secure your own pension. No company or government can do that for you sufficiently.

And for various reasons, putting all your eggs in one basket is never a good idea. So it's also a good idea to diversify your passive income sources.

If dividend stocks are one of your desired passive income streams, put only some of your money in one company, even if it has the potential to be around for a long time. Instead, conduct extensive research and select a few blue-chip companies.

Like any other investment, returns can go down or up due to various factors. For example, dividend rates are typically linked to the company's performance during the fiscal year, which can vary.

Once you get this concept of creating your own pension, your mind will begin to expand. You will realize there are countless possibilities where you may apply your gifts and talents to build your future. Simply believe you can find profit in your passions and keep going until you find what works for you.

You will also realize that you can start small. You do not need millions of dollars to start your passive income journey, and you do not need to shoot for earning millions of dollars passively by a certain deadline. This kind of mindset discourages many beginners from even getting started.

You can start a new venture with very little money, and if

you scale properly, you will be able to earn passive income, which you can use to reinvest or start another stream of income.

Once your passive income consistently surpasses your expenses, your Personal Pension is in place. This is the main target: simply build your monthly passive income higher than your monthly expenses. You can start from wherever you are and build to there.

Figure out a monthly passive income target that you can believe in right now, set your sights on it, and begin to take the baby steps necessary to get your pension created so it will be set up by the time you arrive in your golden years.

Once you have an idea, act on it as soon as possible. Always remember that starting *now* is always the best time.

So there you have it, the NEW three-legged stool for modern retirement:

  i. Tax-Advantaged Accounts (TAACT)
 ii. Savings Bonds
iii. Personal Pension Creation

How each person applies this to their life will be different from the next person, so focus on how this applies to you and your household.

In the next chapter, we will continue the conversation we started earlier and help to clear up our misconceptions about debt. Specifically, most people need to learn the difference between bad debt vs. good debt. In fact, is there even such a thing as good debt? We will reveal how even a mortgage may *not* be considered good debt!

The "Oracle of Omaha" Warren Buffet himself says that borrowing money is "a smart thing to do" when the conditions are right, so it requires a thorough exploration.

Lastly, in the next chapter we will also give you some exclusive content explaining how _any person_ (yes, even you!) can get access to capital and use it in a way that is tailored for your future retirement goals, when used strategically.

You don't want to miss it!

～

As we ride in the truck, driving back to the office, Mac and I are sitting in silence.

Part of me blames Mac for putting my family in this situation. If it wasn't for Mac asking for referrals, then tricking me into giving him one, then making it worth $100 for me to come, then this would never have happened.

But as much as I wanted to put all the focus on Mac, I know that there is a major role that I played in all of this.

Mac never forced me to make any of the choices. My frat brothers tried many times to warn me not to go. I even called Uncle Bob to cancel the appointment.

But here we are.

One big cluster of junk, and my uncle ends up in the emergency room getting heart surgery! I try to come up with a variety of ways to curse Mac for what he's done.

Finally, Mac sighs heavily in the passenger seat beside me and looks over in my direction. "Hey Julian, did I ever tell you about someone named Joy?"

Oh brother, here we go. I keep my mouth shut and continue driving in silence.

"Joy was a lady who used to come by the office," Mac continues. "She was kind of like you, she wasn't really interested in working with us, but she just kept coming around because she liked learning what we teach. She was like a high-ranking nurse, so she knew a *bunch* of people. She was bringing new referrals into the office every week."

So what? My uncle just had a heart attack from this information! I think about cranking up the music loud to drown out Mac's voice. I continue driving in silence.

"So one day, after she had been coming to the office for like almost a year, I found out that she wasn't using any of our products. So I was like, 'Alright Joy, you got to get something for yourself. You can't lead a crusade without being the example first.' So we got her signed with a life insurance policy right there on the spot. She was like your uncle's age, maybe in her early fifties... Then literally like two weeks later..." Mac's voice trails off.

He pauses for a while.

I glance over to see Mac staring off into the distance with tears in his eyes.

"She was diagnosed with cancer... Liver... Stage 4..." Mac's voice is cracking. "She died after a month of the chemo and radiation treatments."

I can tell this event is weighing heavily on his heart. "So you're trying to tell me this business can kill people?" I ask, still upset from the day's events. "Or that death happens a lot here.." I rephrase the question, trying to make it sound nicer.

"No, no, well let me tell you what happened after that," Mac catches his breath. "So remember I told you I had just signed her up for a policy some weeks earlier. She had only sent in one payment for like a couple hundred bucks... Do you know her family got paid a death benefit of half a million dollars?"

I furrow my eyebrows, trying to decipher the story, "But she had stage 4 cancer, so doesn't that mean she had cancer before she got the life insurance?"

"I don't know, probably," Mac admits. "But she seemed normal the whole time, and she had been coming around the office for like a year. No one thought anything. And since she paid the first month of her policy, she was covered for the entire medical process. That diagnosis came as a surprise." Mac lowers his eyes, softly adding, "When she died, it was really tough to go back to work as usual. We was all messed up. This just happened last year."

I drive quietly for another mile or two, then ask, "Do you feel responsible for what happened to her? The cancer diagnosis?"

"No, I had never seen anything like that before... But I am so glad we pushed her to get a policy that day," sighs Mac. "I will never forget the look on both her daughters' faces when I showed up to the funeral with two checks for a quarter million *each*. One for both of Joy's daughters. They just lost their mother, yeah, but the trajectory of their finances are changed now because of a decision she made to start with us."

I almost forget that Uncle Bob just had heart surgery, and all the memories of the day return to me. "Well that might have worked for Joy's situation, but my uncle just had heart surgery. This doesn't apply to him."

"Well, maybe, maybe not," Mac rebuts. "If I would have just stayed there and kept going with him a little longer, I could have convinced him to at least get started with a life insurance policy, and if he signed the docs and sends the check today, you never know, we could have made a case to the company that he signed up *before* the heart attack." Mac sat up in his chair, more animated, "And you never know, maybe his heart attack never happens at all today, maybe it happened because of how we left him.. or how *I* left him... with no answers and no solution. If I just convince him to at least get the bare minimum, then he would've had a little more breathing room in his life... Then maybe this heart attack doesn't happen today. Maybe it happens in two weeks, or maybe it doesn't happen at all."

I am still trying to process what this person beside me is saying. *It sounds like you really believe in this stuff?!* "So you really think the answer was to go *longer* and try to convince him to buy a product?" I ask incredulously.

"Yes! Let me tell you, there is a product I am thinking about right now, Julian, where if let's say, the person buys term life insurance for cheap, say 20-30 bucks, and then they have a heart attack like your uncle just had today, then Uncle Bob gets immediate access to 90% of the death benefit. It's called an *accelerated* death benefit. They just came out with this not too long ago," Mac is now staring at me as though he has a new burst of energy.

"Mac, you are ridiculous right now!" I allow my frustration to bubble over.

"Think about it though, Julian, if *you* don't share this with your family, who will??"

I exhale with a heavy sigh and give my head a subtle shake.

Ping

As we drive into the parking lot of Mac's office, my phone sounds with a text message. I grab my phone from the cupholder to read the screen.

AUNT RACHEL: Your uncle just woke up

I breathe another heavy sigh. This time, it's the sound of relief.

9

CLOSE ENCOUNTERS WITH DEBT

"Courage is what it takes to stand up and speak; courage is also what it takes to sit down and listen."

—Winston Churchill

I decide to go back to my regular life and pretend none of this financial literacy meeting stuff ever happened.

I go back to my part-time job, trying to figure out real estate, sleeping in the living room of the frat house, waking up next to a WWE wrestler's cutout. I even call Uncle Bob a couple of times to check in and listen to his good-natured dry humor.

For a couple weeks, everything seems back to normal.

But it wasn't...

I could not get my brain back to normal. It kept nagging me

with thoughts that would never have occurred to me before the literacy meeting.

There was a particular burning question, constantly unanswered in my mind... *How come I wasn't taught anything about financial literacy in college? Or high school??*

I graduated from one of the most prestigious universities in the world. Thousands more young adults are graduating every year. And I'd never seen a course called "financial literacy" in all my days as a student. Even still, after visiting that "too-large" office in San Jose, I recognized the information as something very valuable to my life.

In my uncle's appointment, I noticed that it was a case of *not* having the information. It wasn't as though he had been taught all about financial literacy, and deliberately ignored the teachings. He just didn't have it, and was therefore unable to apply it in the family household.

With him being such an enormous part of my life growing up, I wondered how many other elders and people close to me that I respected were in the same boat as Uncle Bob? One misstep away from a heart attack (or Stage 4 cancer in Joy's case), and suddenly having the realization that they had no idea how to manage their finances. And they are leaving their family in a state of financial disarray.

This is not based on smarts, it's simply because a person doesn't have the right knowledge, or any people close to them who can properly explain this sort of information in plain english (or any other plain languages).

I make up my mind to go back to another financial literacy meeting, whenever they were having the next one. *How to do I find out when the next one is?*

My mind ponders calling Tim. *What the freak happened to Tim?* I hadn't heard back from him since that night. *Maybe try Mac instead?*

I find my phone and realize I've been beaten to the punch. I discover a text from Mac.

MAC: Hey Julian, you wanna make another $100?

Of course I do. So easily persuaded I am.

My mind thinks considerately about who the next referral should be.

∽

AT THIS TIME IN MY LIFE, THERE WAS A CONSTANT GNAWING IN MY side that I didn't know how to overcome. It was a growing pressure that made me feel as though I had no way out except to continue hustling every dollar I could.

As a young college graduate still figuring out the next steps in my journey, it seemed like a mistake that only someone like me could make. But after Mac took me on the appointment, I found out my uncle was dealing with this in his life as well. And my uncle was a well-established homeowner with a wife and mature kids. How could the same thing be affecting both of us negatively?

This money villain, known as debt, can grow out of control and take over lives. It doesn't matter the age, nationality or gender.

But if banks are operating on a variety of debt instruments (like credit cards and mortgages), how have they lasted so long?

The interesting thing about banks is that, contrary to popular opinion, banks don't save money. Banks are only ordered to keep $1 in reserves out of every $9. The rest of the money is kept in circulation (loans and investments) to stimulate the economy.

In essence, banks thrive on a system of debt.

Although the concept of debt was never a pretty subject from what I learned in childhood and the media, there seems to be something powerful about debt that I am missing here, which begs me to ask the question: If this money system has allowed banks to flourish in big cities all over the world, why would I not learn how to use money as the banks use money?

And just like Alice in Moneyland, down the rabbit hole we go!

Does Debt Have A Good Side?

The adage "there are two sides to every coin" applies to virtually everything in life. We live in a duality. There's no evil without good, no up without down, no success without failure, no light without darkness, etc. However, when it comes to debt, most of us have only been taught about one side – bad debt. But wait a second, what about the good side?

If you've ever been trapped underneath a mountain of bad debt, you know how stressful and agonizing it can be. Multiple calls from collection agents each day, astronomical interest rates, late fees, getting outright denied for everything you apply for, debt compounding faster than you can keep up, seeing no way out, thinking about what would happen if you absolutely fail to pay off the debt and have to take it to the grave with you...These scenarios are very real. I've been there!

Bad debt can be overwhelming and cause mental health problems, especially because people are ashamed of their debt and thus keep their financial struggles to themselves for fear of someone thinking badly of them.

According to the American Psychological Association, finances are a significant source of stress for 64% of Americans.[1] Bad debt can rob you of both your present and future by trapping you in a cycle that makes saving and wealth accumulation difficult. It's the trick of trying to keep up with payments when you can barely make enough money to make ends meet.

In Brittany M. Powell's book "The Debt Project: 99 Portraits Across America", she paints a clear picture of the impact of bad debt on our society, with portraits of people in debt across America photographed in their residences.[2] The portraits are accompanied by a brief hand-written message of their debt amount and the story behind the numbers.

The book's featured subjects are in debt for different (but mostly similar) reasons, such as divorce, student debt, medical debt, unemployment, credit cards, high rent in expensive cities, and difficulty finding a job after graduation.

One person who owes over 50k writes: "*I am currently in debt over 50k. My life is so stressful due to my debt. I find that bankruptcy may be the only choice but I am not comfortable with that. Never thought in my life that I would be in this much debt for so long it never ends and I wish it would.*"

Another one named John, who was 50 years old at the time and a business owner, says: "*After building about 30,000 dollars in debt, I filed for bankruptcy. This was a very shameful thing for me. I believe there should be more education on the debt situation in our society.*"

These stories are a reality for a good number of Americans.

The author of the book, Brittany Powell, started the project after filing for bankruptcy for her photography business in 2012. She found herself in significant debt after becoming underemployed following the 2008 economic collapse. Most people whose jobs were affected by the 2008 financial crisis and the global COVID-19 pandemic related strongly to her story.

All of this reinforces the notion that most Americans are only one emergency away from financial hardship. Most of us do not live in an economically sustainable way and don't know much about the debt game either.

While we blame income inequality, higher unemployment rates, rising living costs, and other factors, getting into bad debt only causes more harm. So, by all means, get rid of bad debt and avoid it. We won't go into detail about getting rid of bad debt here because we covered it in Chapter 3. It would also help to re-read our debt chapter in the first book, where we explain how to defeat this money villain.

That brings us to the theme of this chapter: There *is* such a thing as good debt.

Good Debt Versus Bad Debt

While bad debt makes life more difficult, good debt has the potential to increase your net worth or improve your life in some way.

Bad debt is all about pain and sleepless nights, while good debt allows you to dream about a more financially secure future. Good debt is borrowing funds that help you to invest in an asset or venture that has the potential to increase your net worth and generate more income if everything goes as planned.

There are numerous examples of global blockbusters that would have never made it, if it was not for a loan to get the idea off the ground and a steady stream of capital to make sure the idea did not fail after launch.

Consider the brand name companies Starbucks, Subway, Shopify, and Google. What do they have in common? All of these companies required loans and borrowed capital to start.[3] At the very beginning, these start-ups were simply ideas backed by debt. Today, these ideas have changed the world.

Does this mean you should rush out and go get your first loan for your first idea?

No, probably not!

Even good debt carries risk when it is poorly mismanaged. You must have sound personal finance knowledge and understand the money game you are playing, in order to use good debt successfully.

There is a thin line between bad debt and good debt, and you may not find a type of debt that every single person will agree is "good debt". For example, while most people believe credit card debt is "bad debt" under all circumstances, there exists the belief that credit card debt is *good* debt if you can use the cards strategically to earn more income.

As another example, there are many who believe owning a real estate property that you live in is a great investment and thus a good debt to have. However, others believe that the home you live in is considered "bad debt", since it costs money every month and does not provide an income in most cases.

Without getting too involved in the details, the simple idea behind what makes a debt good vs. bad depends entirely on how the debt is used, and the ongoing benefits received from the debt, physically and financially.

We will go through a few types of debt to give a better idea of how each debt could be considered a good debt, or bad debt, depending on the strategy used and the thought process behind acquiring the debt.

Student loans are an interesting case study, because they could be considered good debt *or* bad debt depending how life turns out after college.

In general, more education can lead to higher-paying jobs and increase your chances of finding another job if you lose one. According to the U.S. Census Bureau, someone with a degree earns 71% more than one who holds a high school diploma only.[4]

If you secure a good job after school, you can pay off your student loan in a few years. However, keep in mind that not all degree programs are created equal. Some will get you a job quickly, while others may leave you with no opportunities to work in your field of study.

Business loans are another type of debt that can be regarded as good or bad, since the potential to pay off the debt is based on the future performance of the business. However, the success of the business is not guaranteed.

Whether a business loan is considered good or bad debt is determined by how the borrowed funds are used, and the plan in place to pay off the debt if things take a turn for the worse.

Business debt is a normal process for the majority of companies, as it infuses the necessary fuel for development and growth, but it must be approached correctly.

Another common type of debt product are loans for real estate, especially mortgages.

Historically, a mortgage was regarded as one of the most secure forms of *good* debt because the monthly payments eventually built your home equity. You are then able to borrow against the home equity and get access to the cash when you need it, even if you have subpar credit. In this sense, the mortgage can turn into a revolving line of credit.

However, experts say your monthly mortgage payments should be at most 28% of your gross monthly income. If you get into the wrong kind of mortgage, or something goes wrong with the house, this could turn into a form of *bad* debt.

When making a home purchase, it's critical to read the fine print to ensure that you understand the terms of your loan. The subprime mortgage crisis taught us the importance of understanding loan terms, as millions lost their homes to foreclosure during the financial crisis. During this time, home prices fell drastically, and adjustable-rate mortgage (ARM) loan payments increased.

First Loans Recorded In History

Let's take a look at loans on a macro level from their inception.

No, debt is not only a 19th or 20th-century invention. It has existed for thousands of years.

The earliest loan record in history was found to be about 4000 years old, from a location in ancient Mesopotamia (which is present-day Iraq, Kuwait, Turkey, and Syria region), where farmers utilized something very similar to a payday loan.[5]

In their case, the payday was the harvest season. The farmers borrowed seeds, planted them, and shared the harvest with the lenders as payment for the loan. Farmers would also borrow animals like cattle and repay lenders by endowing them with the birth of a new calf.

There must be a few readers thinking, "Repaying with crops? But what if the harvest was ruined by drought?" This is something many of us are faced with today, with burning lands around the nation. In ancient times, there were many plagues that would ravage crops, or other natural disasters.

In ancient times, if you borrowed seeds from a lender, but the crops didn't make it to harvesting season for any reason like storm destruction, all you would be required to do was wash your debt table clean. And you would not need to pay anything back that year.

All these laws and more were outlined in the Code of Hammurabi issued by the 6th Babylonian King, aptly named Hammurabi.

At the time, the lending of fiat currency (silver) also became popular, but the challenge was that silver didn't multiply naturally like seeds. With seeds, you'd typically harvest more than what you planted which made sharing the harvest with the lender easy. This wasn't the case with silver. Thus, interest charges were introduced.

The Code of Hammurabi defined the price of silver and regulated the interest charged on silver loans. Thus, from thousands of years ago, here we are today, in a world that has developed exponentially in terms of wealth, abundance, connections, and resources.

While our society negatively perceives debt, we must recognize that debt has been, and always will be, an essential part of wealth creation.

In 1920, there were only 10,000 millionaires in the United States.[6] In 2020, that number swelled to more than 22,000,000 millionaires![7] All while the national debt has continued to grow higher and higher!

Let's focus on the good aspects of debt for a moment.

Debt helps a hard-working family with little savings to buy their first home. Debt helps someone who has no money at all to bring a product to market that will benefit an entire city. Debt helps a person bridge that gap between staying stuck in the same place financially, to moving into the next level of development and finding the right partnership, collaboration, and/or association to change all of their lives forever.

The key is to learn how to differentiate between good and bad debt. Debt that only serves to gratify our superficial needs is bad, and can easily turn into mindless debt. Instead, we must learn how to harness the power of debt, use this power strategically, and be smart about how to repay our just debts.

Even though debt can be a pitfall for many when used mindlessly, the honest truth is that debt is the cornerstone of our modern society. We will illustrate this with a few in-depth real world examples.

Debt & Business

Let's first think about businesses. Most businesses begin with debt, and as small businesses grow into midsize and large businesses, they acquire more debt to scale. In addition to paying employees, an injection of capital is necessary for milestones such as launching the business, expansion, growth, research, and development. Most companies simply don't have enough cash to pay for such expenses when necessary.

So should the business owner simply wait until they have the cash to expand and get things going? Should the company delay the product launch, or delay hiring the new staff member, or delay getting the office space, etc., until the business has enough cash saved up to do this without borrowing any money at all?

Most CEOs and Shareholders alike are currently shouting, "No way, José!"

Fortune 500 Companies wouldn't be where they are today without debt. Business loans eliminate the financial obstacles that may prevent a company from pursuing profitable growth, for instance, expanding to a new market, scaling production, or providing new products/services.

How each company uses business financing will be different, but the goal remains the same – making the business thrive.

Keep in mind, as with any other type of debt, you must exercise due diligence when using business financing. It is not uncommon to come across companies with enormous potential declaring bankruptcy due to poor resource management.

Notwithstanding, we can all draw inspiration from established companies that have used business financing successfully to get to where they are today.

One of the best examples is Subway. It is one of the most renowned food chains, but it is only where it is today because of the initial business loan. Fred DeLuca, the founder, asked for $1,000 from a family friend to set up a sandwich shop in Bridgeport, Connecticut in 1965.

DeLuca was 17 at the time, and his goal was not to start one of the biggest fast-food restaurants in the world. All he wanted was to raise enough money to afford his college and medical school bills.

On the first day, DeLuca sold 312 sandwiches, and the rest is history. He not only accomplished his goal of putting himself through college but also gave us one of the best sandwich shops of all time.[8]

Google is another good example. Larry Page and Sergey Brin had great search engine concepts and entrepreneurial skills but needed more funds to develop the company. They were both grad school students at Stanford University (Go Card!!) and worked from their dorms.

The first search engine they created was named Backrub, but it didn't take off until an investor, named Andy Bechtolsheim, gave them $100,000 in August 1998. These funds gave the team resources to bring Google to life. This included upgrading their workspace from their dorm room to their first office – a garage in Menlo Park, California.

The company announced a $25 million equity funding round in 1999 and has never looked back.[9]

We could go on and on, but the stories of a loan changing history would take up the whole book. Search through the historic Fortune 500 companies or even small businesses, and you will discover they are using (or have used) business financing or some other form of debt to get to where they stand today.

Debt & Real Estate

Another common place you will realize this theme is in real estate. Real estate is one of the most capital-intensive investments, so it's easy to see why most houses and land developments are funded by debt. In fact, over 87% of home buyers purchased a home using a loan in 2021.[10]

From professional real estate development firms to individual borrowers, we all usually turn to debt for capital to buy properties. Otherwise, we would need to wait until we had saved all the cash to purchase or construct the building, which would require an inordinate amount of patience, consistency, and self-discipline. Not to mention, property prices are rising at a higher pace than income growth, and the cash amount needed to purchase your desired family home will likely increase over the years.

The average home sale price today is more than $428,000. With such prices, even the most committed of savers find it hard to save up enough money to buy their home with all cash.

Debt & Government

We also know that governments and municipalities are commonly funded by debt.

State and federal governments use debt to cover budget deficits, which occur when spending for the year exceeds the government revenue. These funds are used to finance community resources and infrastructure, among other things.

The U.S. Federal Government commonly borrows money by issuing Treasury bills, notes, and bonds. This is a significant reason why the U.S. National Debt continues to rise every year. The U.S. national debt as of August 2024 is $35 trillion.[11]

Even though this may sound negative, it's not inherently negative (or positive). This information helps to illustrate how our monetary system is built with debt as a crucial backbone. With that in mind, rather than running away from the idea of debt, learn to embrace it to your advantage.

If you learn how to use debt wisely, you can learn how to acquire strategic debt, which will help you build wealth. If you have a clear plan and use the funds responsibly, you put yourself at an advantage.

The most common way of using debt for wealth building is borrowing to invest. The investment could be in a business, property, shares, etc. Using debt for investing allows you to purchase more assets than you could otherwise. After your investments increase in value, you may end up with a higher overall return after you factor in interest and any other costs associated with the debt.

Of course, this is not to downplay the risks associated with debt.

In the same way, debt can increase your net worth when used strategically, it also increases your liability if your funds are mismanaged or the long-term investment returns are non-existent, or not sufficient to cover the loan costs. Also, if you fail to make loan payments due to unexpected situations like loss of income for an extended period, the debt will turn into a burden and bring more stress, rather than freedom.

There is always risk attached to debt, this is why careful study is required to minimize risk, and understand the pitfalls completely. You may also want to have an emergency plan as a backup in case an unfortunate circumstance arises. However, when used properly, debt can help you build wealth quicker, help you beat inflation, and place you in a better situation financially than without it.

As a reminder, be sure to do thorough research about any investment you plan to get into, consult a qualified financial professional if necessary, and understand exactly what you are looking to accomplish. It is also important to understand the potential worse case scenarios and how to pivot to a "plan b" if something unexpected happens.

Realize that this is information is for educational purposes only. I have no idea what your situation is, and am not your financial advisor. Use this powerful information to do further research. It is extremely important to learn about this now, because of the lack of knowledge available on these concepts. You will hear almost *nobody* talking about this.

It is "common knowledge" in our society that *debt is wrong*, and *debt is bad*, so *pay off all your debt*. I mean, who hasn't heard that? But then, secretly, most people in our society are buried underneath credit card debt, college loans, medical bills, tax liens, car repos, foreclosures, and other collections.

It seems we all know what the "best practices" are, to a certain extent, but there is more going on beneath the surface which causes smart and sophisticated individuals to attract some form of debt into their lives.

As mentioned earlier, this is not something to run away from. Debt has completely inundated our government, banking system, and all major corporations. So, is there more to the story than this?

Yes!

There is a whole other side to the story.

BUY, BORROW, DIE METHOD

To find out more about this other side, we must focus on the segment of the population that has mastered the ability to use debt strategically to accumulate more wealth, avoid tax burden, and pass down generational wealth. This would be the *Rich and Wealthy*.

One of the strategies commonly utilized by the rich & wealthy is a strategy coined Buy, Borrow, Die.[12] This strategy allows them to pay little to no tax compared to their massive wealth (which continues to increase year by year). Although this strategy may sound advanced, this is something that any person can do, regardless of income level.

Let's look at each step of the strategy briefly:

BUY

The first step is simple. All you need to do is own or purchase an asset like stocks, real estate, or a business. Once you own the asset, you will not pay any taxes unless you sell it and get capital gains or receive income from the asset. If you own a company, your shares in the company will be virtually worthless in the beginning, but eventually, as the company grows, they could be worth millions of dollars. However, as long as you don't sell those shares or receive any dividends, you won't pay any tax regardless of the growth.

BORROW

Once you've bought an appreciating asset, you can borrow money to fund your living expenses using the asset as the loan collateral. When you borrow, you avoid selling part or all of your assets and hence avoid taxes. The financial system taxes income, and if you are not selling or receiving dividends, then there's no income. A loan is not taxable since you'll have to pay it back. Thus, you tap into the value of the shares (your wealth) by borrowing against them. The beauty of this is you still own the asset and are able to benefit from the appreciation. When structured properly, you may even get a tax deduction for the interest paid on the loan. This is how Elon Musk, Warren Buffett, and Jeff Bezos have managed to amass some of the largest fortunes in history while paying relatively low taxes compared to their wealth.

DIE

The last step is very important because it pertains to generational wealth.

It is well known that upon death, the IRS imposes something known as the "death tax", where your heirs can be taxed up to 40% of your estate. However, this does not apply to the *Buy, Borrow, Die* strategy.

In this scenario, the heir(s) are not subject to capital gains taxes on assets that they inherit. The heir(s) can sell a portion of the assets to pay off any outstanding loans, or sell all of the assets to get the cash. As an alternative, the heir(s) can decide to keep the assets and continue the Buy, Borrow, Die strategy for themselves and the next generation of heirs.

This allows your heirs to enjoy tax-free wealth and continue to pass down assets to each successive future generation without incurring estate tax.

Final Thoughts On Borrowing Money

Notice how when you borrow money, you do not pay taxes on the borrowed amount, whether it's $1,000 or $100,000. The wealthy understand the power of using strategic debt and leveraging assets to win the money game. And this is available to everyone.

Once you learn how to borrow money strategically, you can increase your purchasing power on demand. The ability to acquire debt (also called OPM or Other People's Money in the investment world) can become infinitely more powerful if we learn how to use the debt to acquire cash-flowing assets or use debt to improve the asset(s) we already have.

If you don't feel like debt is necessary and decide that you prefer to use 100% of your cash for everything, you must realize you will lose purchasing power each year due to taxes and inflation. It's a silent thief that you won't even realize has been sneaking into your cookie jar until years later in the future when the damage is already done.

Borrowing money strategically has the opposite effect. This is a strategy that may seem to be adding a burden to you upfront (with an added cost of a monthly payment). However, with responsible consistent practice, you will realize years in the future that your purchasing power has increased.

Here is an example of using all cash to purchase an asset versus borrowing money to purchase the same asset, and the difference between how each method affects your purchasing power over time.

For this example, we will be buying an asset (trampolines), but the asset can be anything (real estate, automobiles, cell phones, mattresses, etc.); this is just an example.

Obviously, the asset would need to be monetized (making you money), and that's a different process, however let's just imagine the trampolines were already setup to bring you a consistent return on your investment.

There are two scenarios: The first wherein the asset is purchased with all cash, and the second, the asset is purchased with debt. The numbers are simplified for easy math.

In the first example, you buy 100 trampolines that only cost $1 each and produce $1 per month in income. (Total upfront investment: $100, Total income: $100/mo)

The monthly expenses to maintain the trampolines are $40/month, giving you a net profit of $60. (Income - Expenses = $100-$40 = $60/mo profit)

Example #1 — All Cash

	TODAY	FUTURE
	$1	$2
Gross Income	$100/month	$200/month
Expenses	$40/month	$80/month
Debt Service	$0/month	$0/month
Net Income	$60/month	$120/month
New Trampolines	x60	x60

In this example, you can buy 60 more trampolines every month.

Now, let's fast forward 5-10 years.

Because of inflation, trampolines now cost $2 each and will produce $2 per month in income. The expenses have also doubled to $80/month. So at the end of each month, there is $120 in profit. (Income - Expenses = $200 - $80 = $120/mo profit)

The question is, how many more trampolines can you buy each month with the $120 profit? More or less? (Profit / Cost per asset = $120 / $2 = 60 new trampolines/mo)

The answer is the same.

You can still only buy 60 trampolines per month, even though you were 5-10 years in the future, and earning twice as much profit as you were before. The purchasing power did not increase.

In this first example, you never beat inflation and are still stuck in the same place, despite making more money.

This is the trap most of us fall into when it comes to finances. We think if we simply save and accumulate enough money to buy and invest into things with all our own cash, we are winning at the money game. But that is not true.

Inflation is a tricky culprit that keeps you in the same economic situation. And years will pass you by before you realize it.

Next, let's examine the second example, which is using strategic debt to acquire the asset.

In the second example, we will buy the same 100 trampolines, and most of the numbers will remain the same. The main difference in this example is, since we borrow money to make the purchase, there will be the added factor of a debt payment which must be calculated.

How do the numbers work out in this scenario?

After buying 100 trampolines, they produce $100/month in income and have $40/month expenses. The only difference is an added debt payment of $48/month.

(Income - Expenses - Debt Payment = $100 - $40 - $48 = $12/mo profit)

So, at the end of the month, you receive $12 in profit and can buy 12 more trampolines.

This doesn't sound very exciting compared to the first example. In the first example, you are able to purchase 60 more trampolines each month. In the second example, it is only 12 new trampolines each month.

Before you declare me insane and shout profanities at the book, check out the rest of the example. Let's fast forward 5-10 years and see how this plays out.

The trampolines now cost $2 each and produce $2/month in income, same as before. The expenses have doubled to $80/month. However, the debt payment stays the same at $48/month.

(Income - Expenses - Debt Payment = $200 - $80 - $48 = $72/mo profit)

Example #2 — All Debt

	TODAY	FUTURE
	$1	**$2**
Gross Income	$100/month	$200/month
Expenses	$40/month	$80/month
Debt Service	$48/month	$48/month
Net Income	$12/month	$72/month
New Trampolines	x12	**x36**

After these calculations, you find that the profit is now $72/month!

So now, even after factoring in inflation, you are able to purchase 36 more trampolines each month with the profits.

In this second example, did your purchasing power go up or down? Of course, UP!

You are able to purchase three times as much of the asset as you were able to purchase before. This would not have been possible with all cash. This is only possible with strategic debt.

Now you understand why major businesses, non-profits and investors alike, spend considerable time and effort trying to acquire OPM before starting any major project.

We are going to keep this as simple as possible, but believe me, this entire book could be written on this subject alone. This example is meant to serve an alternative for what "good debt" can mean when used the right way.

For additional information, including personal stories and insights, read our blog at www.julianpaulbooks.com

You have exactly what you need to get started on your journey to financial success! Believe that you can learn this, align your pieces in the right way, and you will unlock a world that was never available to you before.

Now that you understand how crucial it is to acquire capital and have access to greater sums of money, we will give you one final piece of the puzzle. This subject will bring this picture full circle. Join us in the next chapter!

$$\sim$$

"Have you heard about the Rule of 72?" Mac asks.

"No I haven't," replies Cousin Mitchell.

"This is a formula that shows how quickly it takes your money to double..."

Mac leads this second appointment with my elder cousin, Mitchell, and his wife, Deborah. I can feel the nervous tension coursing through my body. I am glad that the only lines I am scripted to say the whole appointment are "Hi!" and "This is Mac..." since my teeth are chattering, and those words are about all I can handle.

I pray that since Cousin Mitchell is almost a decade younger than Uncle Bob, he will be able to handle this information without any health scares.

"In our company, we also like to explain how taxes work. Do you know about the investment products that are tax-exempt?" asks Mac.

"No... Well the 401(k) is tax-exempt, right?" Cousin Mitchell asks back.

"No, the 401(k) is pre-tax. Let me explain..." Mac continues.

I do my best to pretend I am listening, but my mind keeps wandering... *Should I be happy that I'm about to make another hundred bucks? Or scared for repercussions that could come after we leave...? Their financial ignorance seems kind of personal to be revealed in front of me, maybe I should just wait in the truck...?*

"Do you both own this home? What sort of coverage do you have in place in case one of you were to pass away? Knock on wood..." Mac goes into his routine spiel with a light knock on the dining table.

Cousin Mitchell is responding with similar answers as I heard Uncle Bob revealing in the previous appointment. Deborah is silent and seems completely uninterested, as she gets up from the table and walks out of sight.

"Is this something you want to take care of today?" Mac finally gets to his closing lines.

"Yes, I definitely want to do something...but I'd have to wait until next month..."

I bring myself back out of my trance. *Did Cous just say he wanted to move forward?*

"Ok that's fine, we can schedule a follow-up for next month," Mac responds. "And just so you know, the reason I'm here with Julian is because we're getting him trained up so he'll be able to do this on his own one day..." I clench up inside and do my best not to make eye contact as Mac makes his final appeal. "Who else do you guys know who would benefit from this information? It would really help out with Julian's training..."

"No one comes to mind right now. I'd need to think about it,"

Cousin Mitchell responds similarly to how Uncle Bob responded.

"You know who I'm thinking of, Mitch?" Deborah reappears from the other room, carrying cups and a pitcher of water. "Tommy and Sister Lisa from bible study. I just heard them talking about some of this stuff last Wednesday."

Hold up, are ya'll actually about to refer me to some people?

After thinking for a moment, Cousin Mitchell says, "Ok, try Tommy and Lisa," while taking his phone out of his pocket. "Let me pull up their numbers to give you..."

GO! "Be Like Mitch & Deb"
Share This Info
With Someone You Love

10

EXTRA CREDIT

"There is no end to education. It is not that you read a book, pass an examination, and finish with education. The whole of life, from the moment you are born to the moment you die, is a process of learning."

—Jiddu Krishnamurti

With the first couple appointments under my belt, I decide to run an experiment and set up as many appointments as Mac can handle. This will help me find out who in the world already knows about these basic financial literacy concepts.

For my next appointment, I have Mac sit down with one of my good friends from college, who is studying to become a doctor.

After this appointment concludes, I realize she had yet to learn about any of the financial literacy teachings.

Next, we visit with Cousin Mitchell's referrals, Tommy and Lisa. Brother Tommy is a Sunday School Teacher, while Sister Lisa is an usher and choir singer. They reveal how their lifestyle causes them to live paycheck to paycheck, and they had been praying for an answer before we showed up. They suggest I meet with the Pastor of their church to have a financial literacy night for the community. I can feel the momentum growing.

Next, I have Mac meet with my high school mentor, a retired veteran. It turns out my mentor had the "Old" Three-Legged Stool already in place, due to his persistence and countless visits to the V.A. Office. However, he had *not* yet learned about the financial literacy teachings that Mac revealed during the appointment.

After that, I introduce Mac to the richest couple I know in my family. A meeting that I was afraid to set up, until my esteemed aunt and uncle (frugal savers and wise investors) tell Mac how the basic financial literacy concepts Mac is presenting is new information that they have never heard before in either of their lifetimes.

Appointment after appointment after appointment follows a similar vein. After each appointment concludes, I notice a subtle shift happening within me.

In the beginning, I am fearful and nervous before every appointment, kicking myself for even setting it up. By the end of the appointment I feel a sense of knowingness that the information is a blessing, and encouragement to set up the next appointment.

Initially, it was the $100 per referral that sucked me in (although Mac stopped paying me after a while, claiming I had "reached my limit"). But regardless of Mac giving me a referral bonus, I am now hooked. What started out as a simple side hustle begins to morph into a passion project. It surprises me that as a young, green graduate, I have just as much financial literacy training (which is none at all) as the people we are sitting down with.

I used to believe financial literacy would vary according to age and/or profession. But after sitting in on appointments with professionals from every field, my old beliefs were shattered. We had appointments with parents and grandparents, accountants, teachers, police officers, professors, nurses, engineers, doctors, plastic surgeons, professors, professional athletes, and even a person who worked for the CIA. Eventually my appointments branch out from being people who I knew, to those I didn't know.

We had appointments with 20 year olds, we had appointments with 50 year olds, we even had appointments with people who were in their 80s. Same presentation. Same responses. In fact, it was a surprise whenever a person claimed they HAD heard a financial literacy concept that was being explained.

Although it is great to do these appointments and deliver knowledge, it seems tragic how little we all know about money. My meetings with everyone shows me the same thing, we are *all* financially illiterate. It is as though the system is beating the world, and none of us even knows the game has started.

As my enthusiasm grows for spreading this knowledge to everyone I know, I start to go through my phone and realize there is one person in particular who would find tremendous value in the knowledge, and that was my Aunt Mary-Jay.

But there is just one problem...

I am too afraid.

Aunt Mary-Jay is not politically correct at all. Aunt Mary-Jay doesn't like strangers in her house, even if I am there to invite them in. She embraced her new life after retirement by drinking liquor and cursing loudly in her living room while watching westerns. Tombstone is her favorite movie to watch (on VHS).

She drives a black convertible Mercedes, plays Bingo on Monday nights, goes to Bible Study on Wednesdays, and has a girl's night out on Fridays. She even got featured in the AARP magazine for the work that she'd been involved in during the civil rights movement in California. She'd practically raised me in my younger years, and I look up to her a great deal.

However, Aunt Mary-Jay (I call her Aunt Jay) made it very clear to me early on that she did not care about learning about how money works, especially from me. "Boy, I'm already retired! I got mine! When you gone get yours? HA! Want me to meet with somebody about some money? For What?!?" I can still hear her voice now. Needless to say, I dropped the subject.

But now that I am having some success with the appointments, her name is coming up for me again, and I am torn. I feel like there's a good chance she could curse out Mac for asking about her money situation when they've just met. Plus, I've known Mac to readily bring up death with every person we've met with thus far. Two things I know about my Aunt Jay: 1) She doesn't talk about money, and 2) She doesn't talk about death.

Plus, I had told Aunt Jay that I'd been with Uncle Bob just before his heart attack. But I did *NOT* tell her that Mac was there with me, meeting about money. I hope to never tell her that part of the story (cat's out of the bag when this book comes out).

However, I am also torn because what if I actually have the appointment with Aunt Mary-Jay, she actually allows Mac to do the presentation without encumbrance, and then we find out *SHE* is also financially illiterate?

No, not her too!

I can't bear the thought. I am running out of elders to turn to for wisdom on financial literacy. At this rate, the only person who I'll have left is Mac. *Ugh really...Mac?!?*

Yet, Mac's words are still stuck to me. If I don't have the appointment with Aunt Mary-Jay, who will?? What if she never learns how to use her money better? What if, in her retirement, she only needs to make a few simple changes to drastically improve the trajectory of her finances? Would I be the one to blame for not sharing? For being too scared?

On this particular day, Mac and I had agreed to go on one appointment with anyone that I could schedule. At the last minute, the person I set up for the day cancelled, so I muster the courage to call Aunt Jay to see if she'd let us stop by.

"Heyyy..." She answers the phone.

"Hey Aunt Jay, what you doing today?" I ask.

"Nothing, why!" She responds.

"I am in the area, had a friend that I wanted you to meet."

"What friend?" She sounds very skeptical.

"No one," I lie. "Just me and this guy Mac. We started a business together and coming through the area, wanted to stop by and say hello."

"What kind of business?" Aunt Mary-Jay inquires.

"We can stop by and tell you all about it, right?" I stick to the subject.

"No. I'm about to go get some breakfast right now."

"You just said you weren't doing nothing!" I chuckle.

"I'm not having no strangers taking up my damn morning, talking about some damn business," Aunt Mary-Jay doesn't mince words.

"Just five minutes, please!" I beg. "It's just gone be real quick. You'll be eating breakfast in no time." I try to say whatever I can to get her to agree.

She pauses for a moment, then asks, "What time ya'll be this way?"

"We're heading to you now, be there in 15-20 minutes," I answer.

"20 MINUTES!?!" She yells.

"Yes, Aunt Jay. Do you need longer than that?"

"No, no... Ya'll just better hurry up and make this quick! I got places to be!" Aunt Mary-Jay shouts as she hangs up the phone.

Ok, the trap is set. I breathe a deep breath, and feel my armpits start to sweat.

I am nervous for this one. Good thing Mac is going to be doing all the talking.

As I sit outside Mac's office waiting for him to come outside. I realize I don't see his car in the parking lot. I call Mac to tell him I'm outside the office. It rings. It rings some more. It goes to voicemail. *Where is Mac?*

Ping

On cue, I receive a text message:

MAC: I am not going to make it today. You'll have to do that appointment yourself.

!?!?@$%^#! went my brain.

My heart starts to beat faster.

~

I USED TO FEEL LIKE A FRAUD FOR GOING TO THESE APPOINTMENTS teaching about financial literacy when I didn't even fully understand my own situation.

How can I be confident sharing tips for staying out of debt when I am in debt myself?

How can I tell someone that life insurance is very important when I don't have life insurance myself?

How can I talk about saving and investing money if I am not saving and investing?

These questions racked my mind throughout this journey, and even though I learned many important financial literacy concepts and became a great teacher of the information, I was *not* the best example of what you would imagine when you thought of a "financial literacy teacher".

I made a LOT of mistakes back then. And even today, I still make mistakes.

Fortunately, I am very stubborn.

With every mistake, I've come to realize there is still more for me to learn. Instead of giving up on becoming financially literate or succumbing to the false belief that I know all there is to know about money, I take a very different approach and wonder what more there is for me to learn.

Over the years of applying this knowledge, year after year, my mindset towards money has slowly started to change. As my mindset has changed, my situation has evolved.

When I first started on the journey, stuck in credit card debt, I found out about something called a "credit report". When I first found my credit report, it had names on it that didn't belong to me, addresses I had never lived at, past due bills that I didn't recognize, and much more.

Attached to this credit report was something called a "credit score". I didn't know what a credit score meant, but mines was in the 500's.

That's good, right? 500 is a high number...

Come to find, *no* it was not good. 500's is not a good number at all. And the credit report had names and other data I did not recognize, which are called "inaccuracies".

Although it would take me years to get to the bottom of that, my stubbornness and refusal accept financial illiteracy helped me to slowly grind on my credit report, until one day I found that my credit score had improved all the way up to 790s.

Credit reports are one of those things that may take a year or two to clean up and get fixed to reflect the information you want to see, but with dedication (and a little stubbornness), you can use this report as a building block to accelerate the progress in your financial journey. While most people have a credit report that holds them back, you will have a credit report that propels you forward.

Credit History Matters

So, what's the deal with these credit scores anyway? If you have a few inaccuracies on your credit report, so what? How does this help you in your actual life? And if your credit is messed up already, are you stuck with it?

Credit scores matter more than most of us realize. A bad or non-existent credit score sounds like a door slamming shut on life's "grown-up" accomplishments — a new apartment, a car loan, car insurance for the new car, a mortgage, business credit for your company, etc.

Employers will also review the information in your credit report before hiring you, which means bad credit could also cost you job opportunities.

Picture this: You have a good income and no debts. You are eager to rent an apartment, so you go apartment hunting, find a fantastic place you love, and submit your tenant application. To your surprise, the landlord informs you that you are ineligible for the apartment because you have no credit score or lack a sufficient credit record.

Later, you somehow find another (less desirable) apartment to live in, and this time, the landlord agrees to approve your tenant application! But there's one condition: you must pay six months of rent in advance. You can't afford six months of rent upfront and don't have a cash stash that you can access, so you're back to square one.

Wait, whaaat?? Hang on a second...

Shouldn't having a steady income and being debt-free make you *more* appealing to prospective landlords, lenders, and financial institutions? Aren't you supposed to get accepted for everything if your money situation is secure?

The reality is that being debt-free is not always enough.

When it comes to big financial decisions like renting or leasing an apartment, getting a loan, mortgage, etc., your credit score always comes into play. If you have no credit score or unscorable credit, landlords, banks, and lenders see you as a financial risk and may deny your request.

And on the other hand, if the application is accepted by lenders and insurance companies, they will normally charge higher interest rates and landlords will require prepayments of multiple months' worth of rent, plus a larger deposit.

This three-digit credit score number is an indicator that predicts your likelihood of timely debt repayment. It indicates your credit risk and is thus used as a basis for lending companies and banks to make decisions about credit approvals, terms, and interest rates.

Remember what we explained in the first book – credit and debt go hand in hand. They are intimately connected. You must have used some form of debt to have a credit score.

Your credit improves by wisely utilizing debt. By avoiding debt and never obtaining any loans or lines of credit, you are doing a disservice to your credit score and limiting your ability to access capital when you finally need it.

The difference between mediocre credit scores and great credit scores can amount to hundreds of thousands of dollars over time.

Now that you recognize the significance of credit scores, it's essential to gain a general understanding of how credit scores are calculated.

The FICO Score

Credit scores are calculated using a system of information called FICO. The FICO® Score is the industry-standard credit scoring model used by 90% of top lenders. Let's briefly review it now.

FICO is short for Fair Isaac Corporation, a credit score brand. The company was the first to develop a method for calculating credit scores based on data collected by credit reporting agencies.

FICO was founded in the 1980s to address a significant issue at the time: discriminatory lending practices. Lenders used to consider factors such as age, gender, race, neighborhood, minority groups, etc.[1] Instead, FICO eliminated discrimination by establishing an automated risk-scoring system regarded as impartial and consistent.

Although other credit scoring formulas (models) have emerged since FICO, most lenders continue to use the FICO model.

The FICO website (www.myFICO.com) allows anyone with a reported credit history to obtain their FICO score. But what data does myFICO use to calculate your credit score? Both positive and negative information from your credit report are used to put together your FICO score.

FICO groups the contents of your credit report into five categories when calculating a credit score.[2] Each category has a different weight on your FICO score, as shown below:

- Payment history (35%)
- Amounts owed (30%)
- Credit history length (15%)
- New credit (10%)
- Credit mix (10%)

The percentages under each category illustrate how important a category is in determining your FICO Scores. However, the weight of each category can vary from person to person based on the information on your credit report.

It's also worth noting that you may have different FICO scores at a given time. Since there are three major credit data collection agencies (Experian, Equifax, and TransUnion), these credit reporting agencies may have different credit data at times. As a result, your FICO scores may differ depending on which agency's data is used to calculate it.

FICO also has variants of its credit scoring formula tailored to various lenders, such as home loans, car loans, etc. This means you will have multiple FICO scores, even if they are all calculated from the same credit reporting agency's data.

Blame This All On Edwin

If you find the whole credit reporting thing complicated and punishing, blame it on the old settlers who did not handle their finances very well, such as Edwin. This is how the need for credit reporting came about many years ago.

During our country's early years, general stores allowed community members to purchase items on credit. Store owners would use pen and paper to keep track of their customers' debts and repayments. And, people returned to pay off the store owners, except Edwin. He never would repay.

One early morning, some of the town's business people gathered over coffee to discuss business. One general store owner mentioned an issue he was having with one of his customers, Edwin. He failed to pay his previous month's bill. Another merchant said he had a similar experience with Edwin.

The other merchants had not done business with Edwin. But they made note of it, and decided if Edwin came into one of their stores, he'd be limited to cash purchases. So Edwin was an example of what it meant to have "bad credit".

Merchants recognized the importance of sharing information as a result of that meeting. They agreed to keep track of and share information about their problematic customers. As the list of people like Edwin grew longer, and it became necessary to document them, the first "credit report" was born.

Credit Visibility

Credit reporting is done to remove consumers from being "credit invisible". Credit invisible simply means you have no credit history at all. When you're credit invisible, none of your bills or expenses are reported to the credit bureaus. This is often the case for people who have never owned a credit card and prefer to pay for everything in cash, even large purchases.

Lacking credit visibility doesn't imply a low credit score. It means there is no credit score at all because there is no credit report from which to calculate the figure. Here's how FICO groups credit scores:

- Exceptional: 800+
- Very Good: 740 to 799
- Good: 670 to 739
- Fair: 580 to 559
- Poor: 580 or less

Since there is no universal starting point for those building credit for the first time, you will not be automatically placed in the poor range. You have no credit score, hence the term "credit invisible". And if you don't have enough credit records to generate a credit score, you will be labeled "unscorable."

One Major Credit Caveat

Now that we've established that you need credit to build credit, there's one major caveat. If you use *too much* of your available credit, it's also bad.[3] This is called *credit utilization*. Credit utilization is the percentage of your overall debt portfolio that you are using at one time.

Remember that 30% of your FICO® Score is judged by the amounts you owe on your credit accounts. This is not surprising, given that the amount you owe influences your ability to make timely payments. As your balances grow, so does the likelihood of being unable to make the monthly payments on time.

Although credit utilization is only part of what determines your credit score, it's an important category to consider because that's where pitfalls can happen. We need debt to have "credit," but if we use too much of our available "credit," we come across as irresponsible borrowers to the lender, and our credit rating decreases. Thus, you must keep your personal credit utilization in check.

Since credit utilization is a significant factor in your credit score, it pays to keep an eye on it. You can easily calculate your credit utilization by dividing the balance by your credit limit. For example, let's say your balance is $250, and your credit limit is $1,000, which is 250÷1000. Your credit utilization is 25%.

Financial experts recommend 30% credit card utilization max. To be safe, it's better to keep your balances below 25% in case of any potential accounting errors. You should always view the 30% rule as a guideline rather than a rule of thumb.

To put yourself in the *Exceptional* category, maintain a credit utilization below 1%, as the FICO scoring model shows that consumers with 800 scores use less than 10% of their utilization each month on average. Using this as a blueprint for obtaining high scores, make it a goal never to use more than 10% of your utilization.[4]

As an additional tip, owning several credit cards with low balances is preferable to having one or two maxed-out cards. Keeping your credit utilization low matters even if you aren't able to pay the balance in full each month.

Building Credit From Scratch

If you have no credit history and want to begin building credit, you are not without options and are not alone. The Consumer Financial Protection Bureau (CFPB) estimates that there are about 26 million "credit invisibles" in the United States. That equates to roughly one out of every ten adults.

According to the same organization, approximately 19 million Americans are "unscorable." If you are in the credit invisible or unscorable category, there are a few places you can start to build your credit so that banks will be lining up to lend you money. You can utilize these strategies even if you are a student or a young professional without a steady income.

Although it may appear frustrating when you begin your credit-building journey, the best part is that you're starting on a clean slate. You haven't done anything negative to your credit profile, and you will be able to begin responsibly and avoid being suckered into bad decisions.

Here are the credit-building strategies[5] you can try:

- Open a secured credit card
- Start a credit-builder loan
- Find a cosigner with good credit
- Become an authorized user on your relative's high-limit credit card

Open a secured credit card

Without a credit score, you have no proof of credit management experience, which is why most lenders avoid such potential clients. But how can a person ever get good credit if they aren't able to obtain credit for the first time?

Lucky for you, a secured credit card is a great way to shortcut this issue. A secured credit card reduces the bank's risk, since the credit card is "secured" by the physical cash as a security deposit. If the borrower doesn't pay their credit card bill, the bank can simply keep the collateral.

This safety net allows lending institutions to offers this product freely to those with poor credit or no credit history. Also, it allows the borrower to get a credit limit based on how much cash was given as the deposit.

If you have a lot of cash that is already sitting in the bank, consider using a portion of it to obtain a secured credit card with a higher limit (over $15,000). Having a higher credit limit will boost your credit profile, and encourage future lenders to approve you for limits that are higher than (or equal to) your secured limit.

Getting a secured credit card will affect your credit score in a variety of ways, namely:

- **Credit utilization ratio**
- **Credit mix**
- **The average age of your accounts**

The main priority, however, is to establish a good payment history. Overall, your payment history accounts for 35% of your FICO score, making it one of the most influential factors on your credit. And since the secured credit card is identical to borrowing funds from yourself, there is a higher likelihood that you will maintain great payment history with this product.

Use this card responsibly for small purchases, pay it off in full each month, and keep your utilization ratio low. Continue to make responsible decisions with all of your other credit-related activities/choices, and you will notice the secured credit card will add a tremendous boost to your credit profile over time.

· · ·

A credit builder loan is a loan specifically designed to build your credit score. For that reason, these loans do not require you to have a credit history or a good credit score. The main thing you need to get approved is sufficient income for the loan amount.

Here's how it works: you apply for the loan, your request is approved, the borrowed amount is held in a bank account while you make payments, and the borrowed amount is released to you once you have fully paid it.

Since you will be able to access the funds once you pay off the loan in full, you can look at it as an opportunity to practice your money-saving habits. The funds that are sent as savings provide a growing security deposit for the lender, and once this process is completed successfully, the lender will be much more comfortable lending unsecured funds to you in the future.

You will find these types of credit builder loans in your smaller financial institutions, such as credit unions and community banks. You can also check out the company CreditStrong, which handles the entire process online for a seamless experience. This lender reports your payments to all three credit bureaus and is an effective program for those who need to build up their credit profile.

Remember, the key information helping you build your credit with a credit builder loan is payment history which accounts for 35% of your FICO score. Simply make your payments on time, and the credit builder loan will put this 35% to work on your behalf. And once the loan/savings term is completed, you get your money back!

Find a co-signer

One of the simplest ways to build credit is to find a person who is willing to cosign on your first loan/unsecured credit card. A cosigner is usually someone with good income and credit who will put their established credit at risk to help you build yours.

The cosigner guarantees to be responsible for the loan, giving the lender two people who promise to pay, making it easier to get the loan approved.

Keep in mind, not everyone is willing to be a cosigner because if any unforeseen difficulties happen on the loan (late payments, collections, etc.), this will attach to their credit as well, and their good scores will suffer.

However, if you make all your payments on time and all goes well, *both* credit profiles will improve because the positive history will be reflected for *both* co-borrowers. This circumstance creates a win-win situation for you and the cosigner.

A cosigner is not the same as a co-borrower. The cosigner simply assumes responsibility for loans if the primary borrower does not make the monthly payment(s), but does not have equal ownership of the purchases. In contrast, a co-borrower is equally responsible for the regular monthly payments AND has equal ownership rights to whatever the borrowed money was used to purchase, such as a car.

Become an authorized user on another person's credit card

Another easy way to build your credit profile is to become an authorized user on another person's credit card. As an authorized user, the credit card limits, age, and other history will be shown on your profile. Even though you are not responsible for repayments as an authorized user, the payment history will also show on your profile.

With the right authorized user card(s), you can boost your credit profile dramatically within just 30-60 days. With this strategy, you can benefit from the primary cardholder's good credit habits and improve your credit scores.

Obviously, you want to make sure the primary cardholder has 100% positive history with the card issuer for the maximum benefit, otherwise you will be inadvertently adding negative history to your credit profile.

It is important to note that not all card issuers report credit activity for authorized users to the credit bureaus. Check with the card issuer beforehand to make sure the primary cardholder's account activity will also be added to your credit profile with all three bureaus as an authorized user. You can usually find this information online when searching credit-building forums, such as the *myFICO Forums*.

WRAPPING IT ALL UP

I'm sure you're wondering how long it will take to establish good credit using these methods. The truth is that the improvement you will see in your score varies per each individual profile. However, each of your credit scores WILL improve with dedicated time and financial discipline.

You won't get an 850 overnight, but focusing on the behaviors that affect your scores will usually result in dramatic improvements within six months or less.

A valid FICO score requires at least one account open for six months or more on your credit report. Within the last six months, your credit activity must have been reported to at least one of the three major credit bureaus.

This period of credit building will assist you in developing the habits that will allow you to maintain good credit in the long run. The better your credit gets, the easier it becomes to access larger lines of capital, and accomplish greater goals.

Access to capital may not seem to be a worthwhile aim for someone just starting their financial journey. But the further you progress on this path, you will realize the importance of having access to funding. You will learn how to use it to your advantage to maintain a steady income in times of need, and accelerate the growth of your net worth when the borrowed money is used methodically in ways that are both responsible and strategic.

~

"So where's this guy you wanting me to meet?"

"He couldn't make it today," I am standing in the foyer of my Aunt Mary-Jay's house wearing a business suit on a Tuesday afternoon. She already knows something is up. I fumble with the briefcase in my hand, trying to find my presentation notes.

"So what you come over here for JP?" Aunt Jay asks me with one of her pointed stares, looking me up and down. "You know bible study ain't till tomorrow. What you dressed up for?"

My armpits are still wet, plus my hands feel clammy. I realize I've never told her about Mac, the office, the financial literacy seminars, nothing. Also, I've never been to any appointments without Mac. *So how do I start?* "Have I mentioned that I've been learning about financial literacy?"

"Financial what?" She asks.

"Financial literacy," I repeat.

"You said literacy?" she repeats more slowly.

"Yes, literacy!" I burst.

"Uhh no...you ain't mention nothing about that," she responds with a curious look, shaking her head. "What about it?"

"Oh nothing, I just wanted to tell you about it," I say meekly, still fumbling around with my briefcase.

"Tell me about what?!?"

"Financial literacy, remember?"

"What you looking for?" Aunt Mary-Jay is now noticing my fumbling around.

"Trying to find my notes," I think I left my notes in the car. *How did I forget my notes?!*

"Notes for what?" Aunt Jay is still staring at me.

"The presentation," I confess, as the briefcase slips out of my hand. I catch it before it hits the ground, but the sudden movement flings my pens and loose papers into the air. Random papers scatter all around the foyer.

"Presentation about what??" Aunt Mary-Jay is startled by the pens flying into her glass vases. Thankfully, nothing breaks as she continues her line of questioning.

"Financial literacy, Aunt Jay!" I wonder how Mac made this look so easy.

"I ain't got no time for no presentation, JP. It's too early for all that. So just tell me whatever it is you want to say." She clearly isn't in the mood. And I am clearly unprepared.

Oh well, here goes nothing. "Have you heard of the Rule of 72?" I ask directly.

"No, what's that?" she steps back slightly.

"It's a formula that tells you how fast it takes your money to double," I bend, set my briefcase down, and pick up random a pen and paper off the floor. "Here, let me write this one thing out for you real fast."

After explaining the Rule of 72 to Aunt Mary-Jay, she asks, "So this is the financial literacy you been talking about?"

"Yes ma'am. I don't know it so well, that's why I wanted you to meet Mac."

"I don't need nobody coming up in here giving no damn presentations," Aunt Mary-Jay shoots back. "I'mma put up a sign on the front door that says No Solicitors!" We laugh together as she makes a gesture above her head.

"Well the real reason I'm here is for referrals," I suddenly remember Mac closing words. "I just want to know if there was anyone you know that could use this sort of information, and if you can refer them to me."

"You called your cousin Tichelle yet?" she asks, referring to her daughter.

"No, I haven't..." Tichelle was living in another state, and I hadn't even considered her.

"Here, I was just talking to her," Aunt Jay says while leading me into the house and picking up her phone. "Let me call her on Facetime now..."

II

PUTTING IT ALL TOGETHER

"Take the first step in faith. You don't have to see the whole
staircase, just take the first step."

—Dr. Martin Luther King Jr.

All the boxes are packed in the back of the truck. It's
really happening!
I stroll to the inside of the frat house for one final goodbye.

Going through my old bedroom/office, which now looks like a
living room again, I take a slow, deep breath. The
entertainment wrestler's cardboard cutout has been moved
closer to the couch. Ever-smiling in bright pink spandex. *I
won't miss you, creepy!*

I walk over to Will and Keenan, sitting in the dining room,
eating sandwiches.

"So you finally moving out, eh?" asks Will between bites.

"About time, bruh!" Keenan pipes up, munching aggressively. "Finally get my couch back!" He laughs.

"Ya'll gone miss how warm I kept the couch all this time!" I joke.

"You know we got somebody else coming right?" Will asks.

This catches me by surprise, "What, *already*?! Who?"

"You know rent is high 'round here," Keenan says.

"Frat just graduated last week, gone stay here a few months," Will informs.

"So this couch won't be cold long," I chuckled.

"Not at all," says Keenan.

"I think he's coming by today..." says Will.

Knock Knock Knock

"...That must be him now!" Will finishes.

We walk towards the front door. I have a feeling of amazement at how quickly they sold my couch spot to someone else. We all share greetings with the younger frat brother, who I remember meeting somewhere in the past.

"You the one that's moving out?" he asks me, as I am getting ready to leave the house.

"Yup, all my stuff already packed," I confess.

"Anything I should know before moving in?" Young frat is sincerely asking.

"Watch out for the shirtless man in the living room," I say while pointing to the cardboard cutout. "He will frighten you out of your dreams sometimes." We laugh.

"What are you doing now?" I ask.

"I don't know, just applying for jobs," he says. "I been thinking about getting into real estate. What about you?"

A smile forms on my face. I think lovingly about the journey I went on to get to where I am in that present moment.

"I started out in real estate, too," I grab my phone from my pocket to add him to my contacts. "What's your number? I got some people I want you to meet..."

$$\sim$$

As you finish up reading this book, remember that this is not the end of the story. This is just the beginning. The next steps are the ones that you take.

May your savings continue to build and increase dollar by dollar by dollar ad infinitum. May you achieve the best credit score that you can obtain. May you have increasing access to capital in every economic condition imaginable.

This final chapter will be a summary of the actionable lessons that we have discussed throughout the book.

Keep in mind, the financial lessons we've covered are not quick fixes; so it's not a question of how *fast* you make these changes. It's about developing the habits through a change in **mindset**. Now you have a roadmap that will help you to develop good financial habits for the long-term in order to autopilot your inevitable success.

· · ·

THE CHECKLIST

By applying this knowledge, you will experience dramatic results within months, and lasting benefits that will be evident within a few years. Take notes on this checklist:

1. **Always pay yourself first**

As explained in the story in Chapter Two, make it a promise to yourself that a portion of everything you earn is yours to keep. After you have developed that habit, ensure that every dollar works to earn you more dollars by taking advantage of compound interest. The longer you have your dollars working for you, the more "offspring" that will be produced passively for you.

2. **Get Rid Of Bad Debt**

It's challenging to build a fortune when you're drowning in bad debt. Get rid of bad debt as soon as possible to recapture your peace of mind. Use at least one tried-and-true BDEP strategy to regain control of your finances: 0% balance transfer promotions, debt consolidation companies, personal loans, and/or filing bankruptcy.

3. **Implement the NEW Three-Legged Stool**

The old three-legged stool of retirement planning is out of your control. Start focusing on incorporating the new pillars, which include TAACT, savings bonds, and personal pensions.

4. Use All Tax Strategies Available To You

Keep in mind that you will pay taxes on all of your retirement investment accounts, so it's not a question of *IF*, it's only a matter of *WHEN*. Do you pay taxes now, every year? Do you pay taxes later, when you're in your 60s? Or do you have an account that is Tax Exempt? These choices will determine how much retirement savings you will have when the "golden" years arrive.

5. Diversify Your Growth Strategies

Your money can grow in one of three ways: fixed, variable, or indexed. There are certain advantages and limitations to each one. For a well-balanced investment portfolio, consider including all three growth structures.

6. Use Bonds Effectively

If you're getting close to retirement, it's a good idea to adjust your portfolio by putting more of your retirement savings in bonds. Other investments are generally riskier, and you have less time to recoup losses. Bonds provide capital preservation, regular income, and an inflation hedge. For a younger person, don't go crazy on bonds. You can afford to take more risks, but still consider investing a small portion of your savings into bonds.

7. Start Your Personalized Pension Plan

Start your own private pension plan to remove your nest egg from the control of external forces, like policymakers. In other words, acquire and/or build an asset(s) that will generate a steady passive income to cover your expenses on autopilot once you retire. This can be something traditional, such as accumulating dividend stocks or rental properties. You can also build something with tremendous potential, such as a monetized YouTube channel, podcast, or other products and services.

8. Use Good Debt

If you wait until you have saved enough *cash* to start a business or invest in anything that has the potential to increase your fortune or wealth-building abilities, the cash will constantly lose purchasing power to inflation and taxes. To combat this, use debt strategically to increase your purchasing power and turn this freight train of momentum in your favor. Instead of fighting against inflation, you learn how to benefit from it.

9. Build Up Your Credit Report

If you are unable to obtain capital because you have bad credit, or no credit (a.k.a. credit invisible), take the necessary steps to build a strong credit score. You can open a secured credit card, take out a credit builder loan, find a cosigner for a loan or credit card, or become an authorized user on someone else's credit card.

10. Continue To Practice & Learn

Remember, money comes in abundance to those who understand the simple laws governing its acquisition. You can work your way to financial freedom at your own pace, regardless of your current financial situation. Your financial goals are only a few decisions away, so take action now if you haven't already. Even just a small step today will make all the difference.

Just take the first step in faith. You don't have to see the whole staircase. Just take the first step. That quote is so good we had to say it twice; this advice had made all the difference in my life, it's worth repeating!

Share a Review On Amazon

Which financial lesson hit home for you? I'd love to hear about anything that has worked for you along your financial journey. Also, what is something you have found out about that was _not_ mentioned in this book? Either good or bad, please let me know. The best way you can tell me how you feel is by leaving an Amazon review for this book. I look forward to reading *your* review and hearing what stood out to you in these pages.

Also, remember to share this knowledge with someone you care about. It is most encouraging to walk this journey together with another person and be a witness to all of the progress you both gain from the subtle mindset shifts mentioned in these pages. Share this as a gift, post a link to our website on your facebook page, and check out our merch store to buy your own wearable financial literacy clothing!

Take care, and all the best to you!

About the Author

Julian Paul graduated from Stanford University with a Bachelor of Science degree in Management Sciences and Engineering.

Soon after graduation, Julian decided to forego using his engineering background and pursue a career in financial services. Julian took on a position with a Fortune 500 company, building an agency under the guidance of a CEO.

After building a team with many clients and licensed affiliates, Julian had experiences where he noticed the financial literacy teachings needed to be expanded in scope. In hopes of filling the void, Julian went to the library and dug up every book he could find on finances and how to manage money successfully.

Equipped with this knowledge and the experience of implementation, Julian put together a series of writings. These writings include a collection of blog posts and newsletters, where anyone seeking to learn about money can gain further wisdom, without the product sales pitch.

Julian is a NAPA Certified Plan Fiduciary Advisor, and spends his spare time learning about the velocity of money. Julian lives in California with his wife and daughter, and enjoys traveling, stock trading, rock climbing, weightlifting, and playing cards.

ALSO BY JULIAN PAUL

Personal Finance For Teens And College Students:
101 Money Secrets You Wish You Learned In High School

REFERENCES

Introduction

1. Klapper, L., Lusardi, A., & Van Oudheusden, P. (n.d.). Financial Literacy Around the World: INSIGHTS FROM THE STANDARD & POOR'S RATINGS SERVICES GLOBAL FINANCIAL LITERACY SURVEY. Retrieved October 1, 2022, from https://gflec.org/wp-content/uploads/2015/11/3313-Finlit_Report_FINAL-5.11.16.pdf?x37611

2. Hornbuckle, Molly. (2022, November 28). Post-graduation readiness report. YouScience. https://www.youscience.com/post-graduation-readiness-report/

Chapter One

1. Eker, T. Harv. (2009). *Secrets Of The Millionaire Mind: Mastering The Inner Game Of Wealth*. Harper Business.

2. Stevenson, Regina. (2021, September 20). Solvency Series: The Role of Risk-Based Capital and Required Reserves for Insurance Carriers. AgentSync. https://agentsync.io/blog/insurance-101/solvency-series-the-role-of-risk-based-capital-and-required-reserves-for-insurance-carriers

Chapter Two

1. Clason, G. S. (1926). *The Richest Man In Babylon*. Public Domain.

Chapter Three

1. Understanding Credit: Good Debt vs. Bad Debt | Equifax. (n.d.). Equifax. https://www.equifax.com/personal/education/credit/report/understanding-credit-good-debt-vs-bad-debt/
2. Livingston, A. (2022, August 9). How to Use 0% Balance Transfer Credit Cards Responsibly. MoneyCrashers. https://www.moneycrashers.com/responsible-use-0-balance-transfer-credit-cards-debt/
3. DeNicola, L. (2019, December 16). How Do Different Debt Consolidation Programs Work? Experian. https://www.experian.com/blogs/ask-experian/how-does-a-debt-consolidation-program-work/
4. Ladika, S. (2022, August 16). How To Get A Personal Loan With Bad Credit. Bankrate. https://www.bankrate.com/loans/personal-loans/how-to-get-a-bad-credit-loan/
5. FindLaw Staff. (2021, June 30). How Soon Will My Credit Score Improve After Bankruptcy? FindLaw.

https://www.findlaw.com/bankruptcy/after-bankruptcy/how-soon-will-my-credit-score-improve-after-bankruptcy-.html

6. United States Courts. (2019). Chapter 7 - Bankruptcy Basics. United States Courts. https://www.uscourts.gov/services-forms/bankruptcy/bankruptcy-basics/chapter-7-bankruptcy-basics

Chapter Four

1. Stanik, B. (2020, October 10). Explaining the 3-Legged Stool of Retirement. SoFi. https://www.sofi.com/learn/content/three-legged-stool-of-retirement/

2. Social Security History. (n.d.). Social Security Administration. Retrieved September 30, 2022. https://www.ssa.gov/history/stool.html

3. Bomey, N. (2019, December 10). "It's really over": Corporate pensions head for extinction as nature of retirement plans changes. USA TODAY. https://www.usatoday.com/story/money/2019/12/10/corporate-pensions-defined-benefit-mercer-report/2618501001/

4. McFarland, B. (2018, February 27). Retirement offerings in the Fortune 500: A retrospective. Willis Towers Watson. https://www.wtwco.com/en-US/Insights/2018/02/evolution-of-retirement-plans-in-fortune-500-companies

5. Yellen, J., Walsh, M. J., Kijakazi, K., & Becerra, X. (2019). Trustees Report Summary. Social Security Administration. https://www.ssa.gov/OACT/TRSUM/index.html

6. Loomis, C. (2004, April 5). The Sinking Of Bethlehem Steel. CNN Money. https://money.cnn.com/

magazines/fortune/fortune_archive/2004/04/05/366339/

7. Paul, T. (2022, February 8). Will Social Security run out of money? Here's what could happen to your benefits if Congress doesn't act. CNBC. https://www.cnbc.com/select/will-social-security-run-out-heres-what-you-need-to-know/

8. Huddleston, C. (2024, May 28). What Social Security Could Look Like in 2035. Yahoo! Finance. https://finance.yahoo.com/news/social-security-runs-program-look-160225816.html

9. Maverick, J. B. (2022, June 8). 3 Reasons Your 401(k) Is Not Enough for Retirement (C. Stapleton & S. Khilhaug, Eds.). Investopedia. https://www.investopedia.com/articles/personal-finance/081315/3-reasons-your-401k-not-enough-retirement.asp

10. Max, S. (2018, September 16). The Inventor of the 401(k) Thinks It Has Gone Awry. Barron's. https://www.barrons.com/articles/the-inventor-of-the-401-k-thinks-it-has-gone-awry-1542413142

11. Emanuel, E. (2014, October). Why I Hope to Die at 75. The Atlantic. https://www.theatlantic.com/magazine/archive/2014/10/why-i-hope-to-die-at-75/379329/

12. Allianz Life. (2024, April 9). Nearly 2 in 3 Americans Worry More about Running Out of Money than Death. Allianz Life. https://www.allianzlife.com/about/newsroom/2024-Press-Releases/Nearly-2-in-3-Americans-Worry-More-about-Running-Out-of-Money-than-Death

13. LaPonsie, M. (2020, April 22). How Living Longer Will Impact Your Retirement. U.S.News. https://money.usnews.com/money/retirement/articles/how-living-longer-will-impact-your-retirement

14. Ward, J. (2024, March 26). "Unretiring": Why Recent Retirees Want to Go Back to Work. T. Rowe Price. https://www.troweprice.com/personal-investing/resources/insights/unretiring-why-recent-retirees-want-to-go-back-to-work.html
15. Ramsey, A. (2022, February 18). Why Your 401(k) Is Central to Biden's Climate Agenda: Explained. Bloomberg Law. https://news.bloomberglaw.com/daily-labor-report/why-your-401k-is-central-to-bidens-climate-agenda-explained

Chapter Five

1. Bogie, J., Michel, A. (2018, April 13). In 1 Graphic, Here's What Uncle Sam Is Doing With Your Tax Money. The Heritage Foundation. https://www.heritage.org/taxes/commentary/1-graphic-heres-what-uncle-sam-doing-your-tax-money
2. Mainstar Trust. (n.d.). Individual Investors Taxable Accounts Page. Mainstar Trust. Retrieved September 30, 2022. https://mainstartrust.com/investor-type/individuals/taxable-account
3. Internal Revenue Service. (2024). Types of Retirement Plans. IRS. https://www.irs.gov/retirement-plans/plan-sponsor/types-of-retirement-plans
4. Armstrong, A. (n.d.). Tax-Deferred Vs. Tax-Exempt Accounts. Advisor's Magazine. Retrieved September 30, 2022. https://www.advisorsmagazine.com/component/content/article/242-feature-article/23840-when-do-you-want-to-pay-taxes
5. Delaware Historical Society. (n.d.). Biography – Senator William V Roth. DE History. https://dehistory.

org/collections/about-our-collections/senator-william-v-roth-collection/biography/

6. Gibbs, S. (2024, March 4). The Best Compound Interest Account [Maximum Growth and Control]. Insurance And Estates. https://www.insuranceandestates.com/compound-interest-growth/

Chapter Six

1. Chen, J. (2022, May 10). Fixed-Rate Certificate of Deposit (CD) (S. Clarine & C. Potters, Eds.). Investopedia. https://www.investopedia.com/terms/f/fixed-rate-certificate-of-deposit.asp
2. Leavitt, L. (2022, May 31). What Is a Variable-Rate CD? (C. Rhinehart & G. LaGuardia, Eds.). The Balance. https://www.thebalance.com/what-is-a-variable-rate-cd-5222632
3. Segal, B. (2017, November 1). Your Guide to Market-Linked CDs. GOBankingRates. https://www.gobankingrates.com/banking/cd-rates/market-linked-cd/

Chapter Seven

1. CFI Team. (2022, January 22). Rule of 72 - Formula, Calculate the Time for an Investment to Double. Corporate Finance Institute. https://corporatefinanceinstitute.com/resources/knowledge/trading-investing/rule-of-72-double-investment/
2. Investopedia Team. (2022, May 25). Treasury Bonds: A Good Investment for Retirement? (A. Smith & K. R.

Schmitt, Eds.). Investopedia. https://www.
investopedia.com/ask/answers/041515/treasury-
bond-good-investment-retirement.asp

3. Vanguard Advisers. (n.d.). How government bonds are
    taxed. Vanguard. https://investor.vanguard.com/
    investor-resources-education/taxes/how-
    government-bonds-are-taxed

4. Loudenback, T. (2020, December 10). Ask a financial
    planner: I'm in my 20s and have a stomach for risk —
    do I need to invest in bonds? Business Insider. https://
    www.businessinsider.com/personal-finance/do-i-
    need-to-invest-in-bonds-20s-2020-12

Chapter Eight

1. Freedman, M. (2005, February 6). The Selling of
    Retirement, And How We Bought It. Washington Post.
    https://www.washingtonpost.com/archive/opinions/
    2005/02/06/the-selling-of-retirement-and-how-we-
    bought-it/742db5fc-4029-4dfe-878f-2ae1383a2bc6/

2. BLS. (2022, September 22). Employee Tenure
    Summary. Bureau of Labor Statistics. https://www.
    bls.gov/news.release/tenure.nr0.htm

3. Buffett, J. (2022, September 19). More Frightening
    Than Death: Fear & Loathing in Retirement. Zety.
    https://zety.com/blog/afraid-of-retirement

4. Money and Pensions Service Staff. (n.d.). Guaranteed
    retirement income (annuities) explained.
    MoneyHelper. https://www.moneyhelper.org.uk/en/
    pensions-and-retirement/taking-your-pension/
    guaranteed-retirement-income-annuities-explained

Chapter Nine

1. APA Press Room. (2020, May). Stress In America. American Psychological Association. https://www.apa.org/news/press/releases/stress

2. Powell, B. M. (2020). The debt project: 99 portraits across America. Graphic Arts Books.

3. Cabrera, E. (2020, December 18). 8 Major Companies That Used Business Loans to Grow. SMB Compass. https://www.smbcompass.com/8-major-companies-who-financed-themselves-with-business-loans/

4. Fay, B. (2022, February 23). Consumer debt statistics & demographics in America. Debt.org. https://www.debt.org/faqs/americans-in-debt/demographics/

5. Amery, A. (2018, October 23). History of Loans: Business Lending Through the Ages. Become. https://www.become.co/blog/a-brief-history-of-loans-business-lending-through-the-ages/

6. Phillips, K. (1991). *The Politics of Rich and Poor: Wealth and the American Electorate in the Reagan Aftermath.* Harpercollins.

7. Ciochia, A. (2024, January 22). How Many Millionaires Are in the US? 2024 Millionaire Statistics. Finmasters. https://finmasters.com/millionaire-statistics/

8. McCreary, M. (2018, May 9). How a 17-Year-Old With $1,000 Started Subway and Became a Billionaire. Entrepreneur. https://www.entrepreneur.com/franchise/how-a-17-year-old-with-1000-started-subway-and-became-a/313130#:~:text=Despite%20his%20inexperience%2C%20his%20youth

9. Hosch, W. L., & Hall, M. (2020). Google Inc. | History & Facts. Encyclopædia Britannica. https://www. britannica.com/topic/Google-Inc

10. Araj, V. (2022, July 6). Pros And Cons Of Buying A House With Cash. Rocket Mortgage. https://www. rocketmortgage.com/learn/buying-a-house-with-cash

11. Adkins, T. (2022, February 14). What the National Debt Means to You. Investopedia. https://www. investopedia.com/articles/economics/10/national-debt.asp

12. Fogle, D. (2022, May 10). Buy, Borrow, Die Strategy: What Is It and How You Can Use It. GOBankingRates. https://www.gobankingrates.com/money/wealth/buy-borrow-die-strategy/

Chapter Ten

1. Kaufman, R. (2018, August 21). The History of the FICO® Score. MyFICO. https://www.myfico.com/credit-education/blog/history-of-the-fico-score

2. Fair Isaac Corporation Staff. (2016). *How are FICO Scores Calculated?* MyFICO. https://www.myfico.com/credit-education/whats-in-your-credit-score

3. Fair Isaac Corporation Staff. (n.d.). How Owing Money Can Impact Your Credit Score. MyFICO. https://www.myfico.com/credit-education/credit-scores/amount-of-debt

4. Schwahn, L. (2016, June 28). How Much of My Credit Card Should I Use? The 30% Utilization Rule. NerdWallet. https://www.nerdwallet.com/article/finance/30-percent-ideal-credit-utilization-ratio-rule

5. Jackson, T. (2021, December 6). How to Build Credit When You Have None. InCharge Debt Solutions. https://www.incharge.org/debt-relief/credit-counseling/bad-credit/how-to-establish-credit-when-you-have-no-credit-history/

www.ingramcontent.com/pod-product-compliance
Lightning Source LLC
Chambersburg PA
CBHW071557210326
41597CB00019B/3279